Young George Washington
and the
French and Indian War

1753-1758

This portrait of George Washington, painted by Charles Willson Peale in 1772, shows him at age forty in the uniform of a British colonial colonel. *Courtesy of Washington-Curtis-Lee Collection, Washington and Lee University, Lexington, Virginia*

Young George Washington
and the
French and Indian War

1753-1758

by
Robert M. McClung

Linnet Books
North Haven, Connecticut

First published 2002 as a Linnet Book,
an imprint of The Shoe String Press, Inc.,
2 Linsley Street, North Haven, Connecticut 06473.

The illustrations on pages 10 and 15 are from *The Planting of Civilization in
Western Pennsylvania* by Solon J. Buck and Elizabeth Hawthorn Buck © 1939 by
the University of Pittsburgh Press, and © 1967 by Elizabeth H. Buck. Reprinted
by permission of the University of Pittsburgh Press.

Library of Congress Cataloging-in-Publication Data

McClung, Robert M.
    Young George Washington and the French and Indian War, 1753-1758 /
Robert M. McClung.
        p. cm.
    Includes bibliographical references and index.
    ISBN 0-208-02509-X (alk. paper)
        1. Washington, George, 1732-1799—Childhood and youth. 2. Washington,
George, 1732-1799—Career in the military. 3. United States—History—
French and Indian War, 1755-1763—Campaigns. 4. Soldiers—United States—
Biography. 5. Presidents—United States—Biography. I. Title.

E312.23 .M38 2002
973.2'6'092—dc21
                                                                    2002016114

The paper in this publication meets the minimum requirements
of American National Standard for Information Sciences—
Permanence of Paper for Printed Library Materials, ANSI Z39.48—1984. ∞

Designed by Carol Sawyer of Rose Design

Printed in the United States of America

For Gale

Contents

	Acknowledgments	ix
	Prologue	1
1.	In His Brother's Footsteps	3
2.	Journey to the Forks of the Ohio	8
3.	Meeting with the Indians	13
4.	The French at Venango	20
5.	Fort Le Boeuf	25
6.	Two Narrow Escapes	31
7.	The French Capture the Forks	37
8.	Shots That Set the World on Fire	46
9.	Fort Necessity	52
10.	The French Attack	57
11.	Braddock Marches on Fort Duquesne	61
12.	A Disastrous Defeat	69
13.	The Long Retreat	76
14.	Blood and Terror on the Frontier	80
15.	Troubles of Command	86
16.	Forbes Road	93

17. Fort Ligonier   102

18. The Fall of Fort Duquesne   107

      Epilogue   111

      Selected Bibliography   115

      Index   117

Acknowledgments

I grew up in the town of Butler, Pennsylvania, about twenty-five miles north of Pittsburgh and the Forks of the Ohio. Much of the action described here occurred in this region. Just a few miles from Butler, the Daughters of the American Revolution have erected a monument commemorating the place where Washington "narrowly escaped death, being shot at by a hostile Indian."

I am deeply indebted to some of my Pennsylvania friends, particularly Paul and Mary Hoffman and Samuel McClung of Verona, and Mary Elizabeth Goehring of Butler. They sent me valuable research material and steered me to many of the places where Washington waged war against the French and their Indian allies.

Particular thanks are also due to the librarians and other staff of the Jones Library in Amherst, Massachusetts, and the Robert Frost Library at Amherst College, who guided me patiently to indispensable research material.

A great many books and papers have been consulted during the preparation of this work. Although all of them provided valuable insight, I found the biographies of Washington by Douglas Southall Freeman and Thomas James Flexner, and Washington's *Diaries* and *Writings*, as carefully edited by John C. Fitzpatrick, to be of particular value.

Finally, I am greatly indebted to my wife Gale for her encouragement, help, and advice during my research and writing of the book and for putting my manuscript into final shape on her computer.

No American is more completely
misunderstood than George Washington.

— JAMES THOMAS FLEXNER
Washington, the Indispensable Man

We know George Washington as the Father of Our Country, the indomitable commander-in-chief of all colonial military forces during the American Revolution, the first president of our fledgling nation, the indispensible leader who, ever since, has been "first in war, first in peace, and first in the hearts of his countrymen."

His portrait stares at us from every dollar bill; his profile graces every quarter. A great western state is named after him, and so is our nation's capital. Seven mountains and nine colleges, as well as countless towns, streets, and buildings all over America bear his name.

His fame endures as our first national hero, but how much do we really know about him as a human being?

Do we see him as a stern, towering general, clad in a resplendent military uniform and with a powdered white wig, as many paintings portray him? Or do we perhaps think of him as that sanctimonious little boy portrayed by his early worshipful biographer, Parson Mason Weems, as telling his inquiring father: "I cannot tell a lie, Pa; you know I can't tell a lie. I did cut it [a cherry tree] with my hatchet."

Both views are equally misleading. In spite of his enduring fame, Washington remains a remote historic figure whose personality, character, and humanity have been obscured by time and the many legends that have grown up around him.

Samuel Eliot Morrison, one of his biographers, notes that "as a young man Washington was impatient and passionate, eager for glory in war, wealth in land and success in love. Even in his maturity his fiery temper would sometimes get the better of him."

Another biographer, James Thomas Flexner, observes that "George Washington was from the first never a follower, always a leader. As a young man during the French and Indian War, he was entrusted with responsibilities beyond his ability to handle. Not only did his inexperience make him militarily inept, but he never understood the wider implications of the situations in which he was involved. . . . In action he could be rash, brash, impolitic, over self-confident. He made dreadful mistakes."

This book follows George Washington as a proud, ambitious young man, unseasoned in war; a youth whose impetuous actions triggered a war between two mighty European nations; a youth who, as he matured, came to recognize and learn from the mistakes he had made.

1.

In His Brother's Footsteps

George . . . quickly made a hero of
Lawrence and began to emulate him.

— DOUGLAS SOUTHALL FREEMAN
George Washington: A Biography

The oldest of six children by his father's second marriage, George Washington was born on February 22, 1732 in Westmoreland County, Virginia. He had two older half brothers and a half sister from his father's first marriage. The head of the family, Augustine Washington, was a well-known and respected colonial landowner, with over 9,000 acres of plantation and other holdings. He died in 1743, when George was only eleven years old. As first son, George's stepbrother Lawrence inherited the largest portion of his father's land and slaves.

As he grew up, George idolized Lawrence, who was fourteen years older, and constantly strove to merit his brother's approval. Lawrence had been educated in

England, and had served as a captain in the regular British army during England's war with Spain, known in America as the War of Jenkins's Ear. In 1741 Lawrence became a member of the Virginia House of Burgesses, the elected branch of the colonial legislature, and was also appointed adjutant general of the Virginia militia, the colony's highest military post. The militia, in contrast to a regular army, was a citizen army which was called into active service only during an emergency.

That same year Lawrence married Anne Fairfax, a member of one of Virginia's—and England's—foremost families. Anne was the daughter of William Fairfax, who managed the Virginia estates of his cousin, Lord Thomas Fairfax, a British peer. After the wedding, Augustine Washington settled the happy couple on one of his holdings, a 2,500-acre plantation on the Potomac River. When Augustine died two years later, he left most of his considerable holdings to his two oldest sons. George was eventually to inherit Ferry Farm, where the family lived, but Lawrence inherited the much larger Potomac plantation and named it Mount Vernon in honor of the British commander he had served under, Admiral Edward Vernon.

His father's death ended any hopes young George may have had of being educated abroad. Instead of being sent to England for his education, like his brothers Lawrence and Augustine, Jr., he attended a small, unnamed school near his home, where he developed an absorbing interest in "ciphering," and learned the rudiments of geometry. As he matured, he enjoyed all the vigorous outdoor pursuits of the local gentry—horse racing, fox hunting, shooting, and the like. When he was fourteen, Lawrence arranged for him to go to sea as a midshipman with the British navy, but at the last moment his mother, a self-centered and domineering woman, vehemently objected. George reluctantly abided by her decision. If he had joined the British navy, the whole course of American history might have been dramatically different.

In his late teens, George stood more than six feet tall. He had reddish-brown hair and big hands and feet that sometimes made for youthful clumsiness in his eagerness to perform. He enjoyed mathematics and, by the time he was seventeen, became a competent surveyor. His eminent neighbor, Lord Fairfax, employed him to survey some of his land holdings.

In the winter of 1748-49, Lawrence developed a disturbing cough, the forerunner of a continuing and life-threatening disease—evidently tuberculosis. Accompanied by George, he sought a cure in warm springs across the Blue Ridge Mountains (now Berkeley Springs, West Virginia). After his stay at these curative waters, Lawrence felt so much better that he accepted the presidency of the Ohio Company, a corporation of prominent English and Virginian businessmen who had been given a charter by King George II for a half-million acres of wilderness lands west of the mountains and south of the Ohio River. The company aimed to survey, settle, and develop these lands and make a handsome profit for everyone concerned.

Lawrence's health continued to deteriorate, however, in spite of a return to the warm springs with George, and a trip to the West Indian island of Barbados, with the hope that a stay in the tropics might improve his condition. Nothing helped. In July, 1752, he died at Mount Vernon.

The death of Lawrence was a cruel blow to twenty-year-old George, but with the thought of following in his brother's footsteps, he met with Virginia's governor, Robert Dinwiddie, in Williamsburg, and expressed his desire to become an adjutant—an administrative staff officer—of Virginia's militia, as Lawrence had been. The governor complied, appointing George an adjutant of

one of the colony's four military districts, with the rank of major
and a salary of 100 pounds a year.

Dinwiddie, a plump and benevolent-looking Scotsman, was already
one of the principal members of the Ohio Company when he
arrived in Virginia to assume his position as lieutenant governor of
the colony in November, 1751. As acting governor, he soon
received reports of disquieting French activity in the Ohio country
to the north, a region claimed by both Great Britain and France.

From the seventeenth century on, both of these countries had
vied with one another for dominance and control of most of North
America north of Mexico and other Spanish holdings. England's
thirteen colonies rimmed the eastern seaboard from Massachusetts
to Georgia, but Britain also claimed vast stretches of land to the
west of the Allegheny Mountains and in the Ohio Valley. France,
for her part, regarded the Ohio Valley and much of the interior of
the continent to the north and west as French possessions, basing
her rights on French explorer Robert Cavalier Sieur de La Salle's
descent of the Mississippi to the Gulf of Mexico in 1682, when he
claimed the whole valley for France and named it Louisiana in
honor of King Louis XIV.

The Marquis Duquesne arrived in Quebec as governor of
New France, as this vast territory was called, in the summer of
1752, just a few months after Dinwiddie had arrived in Virginia.
He immediately set about strengthening French claims to the disputed lands. In the spring of 1753 he sent 1,500 men in a great
fleet of canoes and cargo boats loaded with supplies west on Lake
Ontario and then by portage to Lake Erie. There the French
forces built a new fort at Presque Isle, about a hundred miles as the
crow flies north of the Forks of the Ohio, where the Allegheny and

Monongahela rivers join. They then built a portage road from Presque Isle to French Creek, which flows into the Allegheny, and built another fort there—Fort Le Boeuf.

But this was just the beginning. Heading down the Allegheny, the French seized and occupied a colonial trading post at Venango, where French Creek joined the Allegheny River. It would become Fort Machault. They were thus poised to head southward in force the following spring to solidify their claim to the Forks and the Ohio River lands beyond.

Outraged by this French activity in a region that he considered rightfully Virginia's and England's, Governor Dinwiddie dispatched several impassioned reports to London, describing what was happening and asking for instructions from the king.

In October His Highness replied, stating that Virginia should build forts on the Ohio, and send an official messenger to the northern wilderness to discover all he could about French activities on land claimed by the English. If they were indeed trespassing, the messenger should "require of them peaceably to depart." If they refused, King George II wrote, "we do strictly command and charge you to drive them out by force of arms."

Dinwiddie had the reply he wanted. Now he could act. He promptly drafted a letter warning the French to get out of the Ohio Valley, and commissioned his recently appointed military adjutant, George Washington, to carry the message to the French. The date was October 31, 1753.

The messenger was just twenty-one years old, and his decisions and actions during and after his fateful journey would set off a world war between the two European powers.

2.

Journey to the Forks of the Ohio

The land in the forks I think
extremely well situated for a fort. . . .
— GEORGE WASHINGTON
Journal

"I was commissioned and appointed by the Hon. Robert Dinwiddie, Esq.; Governor of Virginia, & c., to visit and deliver a letter to the Commandant of the French forces on the Ohio," Washington wrote in his journal, "and set out on the intended Journey the same day." The young major had volunteered for the assignment and was elated to have been chosen to carry the message to the French. Proud and ambitious, sure of his own abilities, Washington knew that this was a rare opportunity to advance his dreams of being a leading man in the affairs of Virginia.

Arriving in Fredericksburg the next day, he hired a young Hollander, Jacob van Braam, as his interpreter in his dealings with the French. Van Braam was Washington's former fencing master; he had been a lieutenant in the Dutch army, and had a good knowledge of French. His mastery of English, however, was meager, which later would prove near-disastrous for Washington.

The two proceeded to Alexandria, where Washington purchased some of the supplies and equipment they would need for the wilderness journey; then on to Winchester where pack and riding horses and additional equipment were secured. They traveled on to Wills Creek in the Shenandoah Valley, just to the east of the Allegheny Mountains. There the Ohio Company had built a stronghouse—a sturdy log-and-timber building two stories high, with ample room to store supplies needed for trading with the Indians, and with living quarters for an Ohio Company agent. Soon it would be fortified and called Fort Cumberland.

Christopher Gist, a well-known frontiersman and Indian trader, had a cabin nearby. He had performed various services for the Ohio Company, and had represented it at Logstown, an Indian settlement on the Ohio, when the company had bargained with the Indians, promising them a storehouse and trading post at the Forks in exchange for Indian land grants south of the Ohio River.

In his mid-forties, Gist was strong, reliable, and skilled in negotiating with the various Indian tribes. Dinwiddie had given Washington a letter for Gist, asking him to join the expedition to the French. The frontiersman quickly accepted. His experience and knowledge of the wilderness were to prove invaluable in the days to come.

Wills Creek was the advance post for travelers setting forth into the unsettled wild lands ahead. It was here that Washington hired four hardy backwoodsmen as hunters, camp attendants, and horse wranglers. In his journal he rather condescendingly called them "servitors." They were Indian traders Barnaby Currin and John MacQuire and frontiersmen Henry Steward and William Jenkins.

On November 15 the party of seven set out from Wills Creek, with Gist as guide on the journey to the Forks of the Ohio and the French forts beyond. All ahead was wilderness country—a region of vast forests, swamps, and tangled underbrush, with rugged mountains and many swift-flowing streams to cross, and winter on the way. As one unhappy British soldier remarked a couple of years later, it was "a desolate country uninhabited by anything but wild Indians, bears, and rattlesnakes." With the coming of winter, the rattlesnakes were hibernating, and the bears going into their winter quarters, but the bitter cold, the rain, snow, and ice were all difficulties to be faced, not only by the men but also by the horses loaded down with camping gear and supplies.

A pack-horse train carries supplies through the wilderness. *Courtesy of the University of Pittsburgh Press*

Thirty-five miles from Wills Creek, they forded the Youghio-gheny River and started the difficult ascent of one of the Allegheny mountains, the so-called Laurel Hill. This rugged and densely forested chain of highlands rose 2,400 feet, then sloped down-ward to a broad plateau, the Great Meadows. Another formida-ble mountain chain, Chestnut Ridge, lay ahead. Instead of crossing it and heading for the Monongahela River to the west, they struck north at Gist's advice, following a path between the snowy mountains.

For the next several days the weary travelers slogged their way onward, driving their little band of pack horses ahead of them. They crossed the Youghiogheny once again and endured more rain and wet snow. Gist killed a deer and they feasted on fresh venison when they made camp at nightfall.

On November 22 they reached the Monongahela River at the mouth of Turtle Creek, where John Frazier, a well-known Indian trader, had a cabin. Less than a year before, Frazier had operated a thriving trading post at Venango. The previous spring, however, a force of French soldiers had come down from Lake Erie and taken over the post.

Frazier had some disturbing news for Washington and his party. He informed them of recent French activity in the Ohio country, and said that three nations of Indians had decided to cast their lot with the French. He had also learned that the com-manding officer at Fort Le Boeuf, Pierre Paul Marin, had just died after a long illness, and most of the French forces had now gone north into winter quarters.

Frazier's cabin was just ten miles south of the Forks. The waters of the Monongahela were very high at this time, and "quite impassable," Washington noted, "without swimming our horses." The trader, however, obligingly lent the travelers a canoe so that

Washington could send two of his men, Barney Currin and Henry Steward, down the Monongahela with their baggage.

Leaving the others to accompany the horses to the Forks, the young major dashed ahead and reached the point of land where the Allegheny and Monongahela rivers met to form the Ohio before the canoe got there.

Viewing the site, he immediately grasped its importance. "As I got down before the Canoe, I spent some time in viewing the Rivers, and the Land in the Fork; which I think extremely well situated for a Fort, as it has the absolute command of both rivers," he noted in his report. "The Land at the Point is 20 or 25 Feet above the common Surface of the Water; and a considerable Bottome of flat, well-timbered land all around it, it very convenient for Building: The Rivers are each a Quarter of a Mile or more across, and run very nearly at right Angles, Alighany bearing N.E. and Monongahela S.E. The former of these two is a very rapid and swift running Water; the other deep and still, without any perceptible Fall."

Meanwhile, Currin and Steward arrived in the canoe with the baggage, which they unloaded on the right, or northern, bank of the Allegheny. Finally the other members of the party arrived with the horses, which were made to swim across the river. Camp was quickly made.

Washington planned to meet with nearby Indians the next day, especially Tanacharisson, the Half-King, as he was called by the English, the Seneca chief who represented the Iroquois Confederacy in its dealings with all the lesser tribes of the region.

3.

Meeting with the Indians

I am not afraid of Flies, or Musquitos,
for Indians are such as those.
— FRENCH COMMANDER PIERRE PAUL MARIN,
speaking to the Half-King

Gaining the support of the various Indian tribes living in the disputed Ohio country was of vital importance to both the English and the French, as Washington knew. Caught between the competing activities of the two European powers, the Indians had long struggled to maintain their own rights and identities in these lands which they considered theirs. Some tribes favored the English, some the French.

The most powerful of all the Indian nations were the six tribes that formed the Iroquois Confederacy—the Mohawk, Oneida, Tuscarora, Onondaga, Cayuga, and Seneca—all of them sandwiched between the French to the north and the English to the south and east. The Iroquois dominated all the lesser tribes around them, including the Delaware, Shawnee, Miami, Wyandot, and others of the Algonquin family. The Six Nations had long sought to be neutral in the British-French rivalry, but were finding such a position more and more difficult to maintain.

Governor Dinwiddie had given Washington explicit instructions to meet with friendly Indian chiefs at Logstown, an Indian village eighteen miles downriver from the Forks of the Ohio. He was to assure them of British friendship, to get from them all the information he could about the French, and to ask them for an Indian escort for the trip north to deliver the governor's letter.

Washington first called on a friendly Delaware leader, Chief Shingiss, who lived just two miles downstream from the Forks. He invited him and a lesser Indian leader, Chief Lowinolach, to accompany him to Logstown to confer with the Half-King and other Indians there. The two readily agreed, and the party set off immediately, reaching Logstown about sundown.

Situated on rich bottomland on the right bank of the Ohio, Logstown consisted of a number of huts and a large longhouse where the Indians customarily met for their councils. When they arrived, Washington recruited an Irish trader there, John Davison, as his interpreter in talks with the Indians. They first met with Monakatoocha, a chief second only to the Half-King in importance, and learned from him that the Half-King was at his hunting cabin on Little Bear Creek, some fifteen miles distant.

After giving Monakatoocha some wampum and a twist of tobacco, the young Virginian asked him to send a messenger to the Half-King requesting him to attend a council as soon as possible. Monakatoocha promised to send a runner to the Half-King the next morning.

The Seneca Half-King, Chief Tanacharisson, arrived at Logstown the following afternoon, and Washington immediately called

Iroquois longhouses were constructed with bark over a framework of poles. The woman at the left is grinding corn; the one in the center is roasting ears of corn; and the woman at right is putting food into an open pit where corn and other supplies are stored. *Courtesy of the University of Pittsburgh Press*

on him formally in the chief's cabin. The Half-King was an imposing figure—tall and strong, intelligent and proud. Fifty-three years old, he had been born a Catawba—a minor tribe—but was captured as a boy and reared as a Seneca. He had risen to power as he reached manhood and had been designated as a spokesman for the Iroquois Confederacy in dealing with all the lesser tribes in the Ohio country, and exerting Six Nations authority over them. He hated the French who he claimed had killed his father.

Washington invited the Half-King to his own tent for a private talk. He wanted to get as much information as he could from the chief about French activities and intentions, and about the best route to their forts.

The Half-King advised him that it would be best to proceed via Venango, a journey of perhaps five or six days. He then told

Washington about the outrageous treatment he had received several months before from the late French commander, Pierre Paul Marin, at Fort Le Boeuf.

Recording the Half-King's account in his journal, Washington wrote that "When he went to the Fort, he [the Half-King] said he was received in a very stern Manner by the late Commander, who asked him very abruptly what he had come about, and to declare his Business." The Half-King then went on to relate what he had said to Marin:

"Fathers, we kindled a fire a long Time ago, at a place called Montreal, where we desired you to stay and not to come and intrude upon our land. I now desire you to dispatch to that Place; for it be known to you, Fathers, that this is our Land and not yours. . . .

"If you had come in a peaceable Manner, like our Brothers the English, we should not have been against you trading with us, as they do; BUT TO COME, FATHERS, AND BUILD HOUSES UPON OUR LAND AND TAKE IT BY FORCE IS WHAT WE CANNOT SUBMIT TO.

"Fathers, Both you and the English are white, we live in a country between; therefore the land belongs to neither one nor t'other. But the Great Being above allow'd it to be a place of Residence for us; so, Fathers, I desire you to withdraw, as I have done [desired of] our Brothers the English: For I will keep you at Arm's length. I lay this down as a Trial for both, to see which will have the greatest Regard for it, and that Side we will stand by, and make equal sharers with us. Our Brothers, the English, have heard this, and I come now to tell it to you; for I am not afraid to discharge you off this Land."

Marin, tired and terminally ill, had replied harshly to the Half-King's speech, evidently seeking to humiliate the sachem. "I am not afraid of Flies, or Musquitos, for Indians are such as those. I tell you, down the River I will go and build upon it, according to my command. If the River was block'd up, I have forces sufficient to burst it open and tread under my Feet all that Stand in Opposition, together with their Alliances; for my Force is as the Sand on the Sea Shore; therefore, here is your Wampum. I fling it at you. Child, you talk foolish; you say this Land belongs to you, but there is not the Black of my Nail [the dirt under his fingernails] yours. . . . It is my Land, and I will have it, let who will stand-up for, or say—against it."

Marin's abusive words and his scornful action in flinging the wampum treaty belt at the Half-King clearly indicated that the French commander was deliberately and contemptuously making an eternal enemy of the Seneca chief.

Among Indian nations it was the custom to exchange wampum treaty belts with each other or with European powers when a formal agreement or treaty was established between them. The return of a treaty belt signified a termination of the agreement.

Marin had died soon after their ill-fated meeting, but that made no difference to the Half-King. He would now do everything in his power, he vowed, to help the English against the French.

The Half-King's speech made it clear, however, that the Indian view of land ownership was very different from that of the Europeans, whether British or French. The Indians would cooperate with traders who bought their furs and sold them needed supplies, but they would take a dim view of any whites who came claiming land ownership and staking out settlements.

Continuing his account, the Half-King described to Washington the two new forts the French had built that summer and fall: Fort Presque Isle on the southern shore of Lake Erie, and Fort

Le Boeuf, sixteen miles inland, on the bank of French Creek, with a wagon road cleared between them for the transportation of supplies and men.

After this important private meeting with the Half-King, Washington bade farewell to his ally, saying that he would talk to all the Indian leaders in the longhouse the next day.

The following morning the young adjutant greeted the assembled chiefs and addressed them formally about the purpose of his mission. "Brothers, I have called you together in Council by order of your Brother, the Governor of Virginia, to acquaint you, that I am sent, with all possible Dispatch, to visit and deliver a Letter to the French commandant, of very great Importance to our Brothers, the English; and I dare say to you their Friends and Allies."

Although Washington didn't explain what was in the governor's letter, the Half-King strongly supported his words, and said that the Indians would provide an escort for the party, as Washington had requested. He then asked for a delay of three days while he arranged a proper escort and retrieved from his hunting cabin the wampum treaty belt the French had given him some time before. He wanted to return it with a formal speech to signify a termination of all previous agreements between them.

Washington was eager to go on as quickly as possible, but he reluctantly agreed to wait. After retrieving his wampum belt the next day, the Half-King, Monakatoocha, and two other Indian leaders came to Washington to ask what exactly was his purpose in visiting the French. What did the governor's letter say? Washington was loath to give any specifics, since the letter ordered the French to get out of the Ohio Valley because the British claimed it. The Indians, however, considered it *their* land, as Washington knew. He answered them in very general terms, which, he later noted, "allayed their curiosity a little."

Monakatoocha then told Washington how the French commander at Venango, Captain Philippe Joncaire, had summoned all the neighboring Indians to a council. He had told them that the approaching winter had prevented the French from coming down the Allegheny in the fall, but they would come in great force in the spring. Joncaire had warned the Indians to take no part in what would happen, for he expected a long war with the English.

It was evident to Washington that a number of the tribes that the Half-King dealt with were not in agreement about siding with the English. Many of them did not want to turn in their French treaty belts, as the Half-King urged, signifying that their agreements with the French were ended. The British and French were evidently heading for a fight, and the Indians wished to remain neutral, waiting to see which of the European powers would win. They wanted to be on the winning side.

After one more day of delay, Washington and his party started for Venango on November 30, with only four Indians—the Half-King and two elderly chiefs, Jeskakake and White Thunder, and a hunter. The young Virginian must have realized that this small escort, and the Half-King's inability to get other treaty belts returned to the French, were omens of future difficulties.

4.

The French at Venango

They [the French] told me that it was their
absolute Design to take possession of the Ohio,
and by G—— they would do it.

— GEORGE WASHINGTON
Journal

Gist and the Indians led the way, following an Indian trail leading to the French post at Venango. After fifteen miles, they arrived at Murthering Town, an Indian village on Great Beaver Creek. Here they traded for dried meat as well as corn for the horses.

The next day they traveled about thirty miles through a cold, wet forest that enclosed them on either side, the trees dripping water on the horses and men as they slogged their way through dense underbrush and waded across icy streams. The day after, the Indians killed two deer and they were able to enjoy broiled venison at their campfire that night.

On December 4 they reached their destination. Venango, Washington later noted in his journal, "is an

Major Washington leads his men through the western Pennsylvania wilderness, on his mission to the French. *Courtesy of the Library of Congress*

old Indian Town situated at the Mouth of French Creek, on Ohio [Allegheny]; and lies near N. about 65 miles from the Loggs-Town, but more than 70 the way we were obliged to go." Here they saw the French flag, the *fleur-de-lis*, flying over what had been Frazier's trading post.

While the helpers pitched the tent, and the Half-King and his companions went to confer with the resident Indians, Washington, Gist, and van Braam walked over to the French post where they were greeted by Captain Philippe Thomas Joncaire, the commander, and other French officers. Joncaire, forty-six years old, the product of a Seneca mother and a French officer, was an imposing and powerful figure. He was widely known as a leading personality in dealing with the Iroquois and all the lesser tribes and, whenever possible, weaning them to the French side. Half Indian himself, he exuded confidence and the rightness of the French in their claims to the Ohio region. "He invited us to sup with them," Washington wrote, "and treated us with the greatest Complaissance."

Refusing to accept Dinwiddie's letter, Joncaire said that it should be delivered to the commander at Fort Le Boeuf, farther north on French Creek. As the dinner progressed, he and the other French officers spoke freely about the French claims to the Ohio country. "The Wine, as they dosed themselves pretty plentifully with it," Washington noted, "soon banished the Restraint which first appeared in their Conversation; and gave a license to the Tongues to reveal their Sentiments more freely.

"They told me, That it was their absolute Design to take possession of the Ohio, and by G—— they would do it; For that, altho' they were sensible the English could raise two Men to their one; yet they knew their [English] Motions were too slow and dilatory to prevent any Undertaking of theirs. They pretend to have an undoubted Right to the River, from a Discovery made by one La Salle 60 years ago; and the Rise of this Expedition is, to prevent our settling on the River or Waters of it, as they had heard of some Families moving-out in Order thereto. From the best Intelligence I could get, there have been 1500 Men on their Side Ontario Lake: But upon the Death of the General [Marin], all were recalled to about 6 or 700, who were left to garrison four Forts, 150 or thereabout in each."

These four forts were the two recently constructed ones—Le Boeuf and Presque Isle; a small fort at the falls of Lake Erie; and another about twenty miles further east on Lake Ontario. "Between this Fort and Montreal," they told Washington, "there are three others, the first of which is near opposite to the English Fort Oswego."

The next day was cold and rainy, delaying their start for Fort Le Boeuf. The Half-King and his Indian companions spent much of the day conferring with the Delawares in residence at Venango. The local Indians, they learned, were unwilling to cut their ties to the French.

Captain Joncaire, for his part, set out to woo the Half-King and his party to the side of the French. He invited the Half-King, Jeskakake, and White Thunder into the stockade, gave them presents, and plied them with brandy until they were intoxicated, as he had planned. The Half-King had been ready to give his speech to Joncaire, ending the Iroquois and Delaware alliance with the French, but was too drunk to do it.

Early the next morning the Half-King came to Washington's tent. He was ashamed of his conduct the day before, and asked for a delay in starting out for Fort Le Boeuf until he had delivered his speech to the French officers. Washington reluctantly agreed.

Joncaire lit the council fire, and the council assembled at one o'clock in the afternoon. After interminable preliminaries, the Half-King gave his speech and tried to return the French treaty belt. Joncaire refused to accept it, however, saying it should be given to the commander at Fort Le Boeuf. When the council was finally over, Washington returned to his tent, firmly resolved that they head out the next morning.

"Monsieur La Force, Commissary of the French Stores, and three other Soldiers, came over to accompany us up," Washington recorded the next day. "We found it extremely difficult to get the Indians off To-day, as every Stratagem had been used to prevent their going-up with me. I had last night left John Davison (the Indian interpreter whom I brought with me from town), and strictly charged him not to be out of their Company, as I could not get them over to my Tent; for they had some business with Kustaloga [a local Delaware chief], and chiefly to know the Reason why he did not deliver up the French Belt which he had in

Keeping: But I was obliged to send Mr. Gist over To-day to fetch them; which he did with great Persuasion."

Accompanied by the four French soldiers as escorts, the party of colonials and Indians finally set out on December 7 for Fort Le Boeuf, traveling up the east bank of French Creek.

5.

Fort Le Boeuf

I can't say that ever in my life I suffered
so much Anxiety as I did in this Affair.

— GEORGE WASHINGTON
Journal

"At 11 o'Clock we set out for the Fort," Washington noted in his journal, "and were prevented from arriving there till the 11th by excessive Rains, Snows, and bad Travelling through many Mires and Swamps. These we were obliged to pass, to avoid crossing the Creek, which was impossible, either by fording or rafting, the Water was so high and rapid."

The sun had set and it was fast becoming dark when the party arrived at a point of land opposite Fort Le Boeuf, which was on the west side of French Creek. Washington sent van Braam to notify the French of his arrival, and after a short wait several French officers came over in a canoe and invited Washington to the fort for dinner that evening.

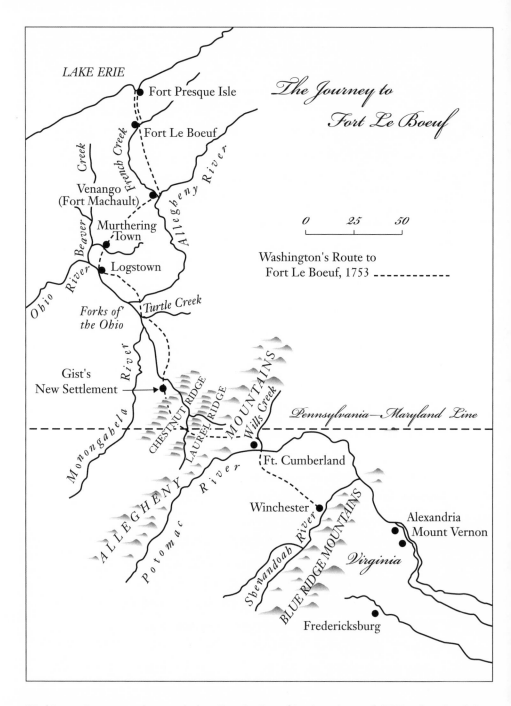

Washington's route as he traveled to Fort Le Boeuf in the winter of 1753, when he delivered Governor Dinwiddie's letter to the French. *Courtesy of the author*

The next day the Virginian noted that "I prepared early to wait upon the Commander, and was received and conducted to him by the second Officer in Command. I acquainted him with my Business, and offered my Commission and Letter: Both of which he desired me to keep till the arrival of Monsieur Riparti Captain of the next Fort [Presque Isle], who was sent for and expected every Hour.

"This Commander is a Knight of the military Order of St. Louis, and named Legardeur de St. Pierre," Washington continued. "He is an elderly Gentleman, and has much of the air of a Soldier. He was sent over to take the Command immediately upon the Death of the late General [Marin], and arrived here just seven Days before me.

"At 1 o'Clock the Gentleman who was sent for arrived, when I offered the Letter, &c again; which they received, and adjourned into a private Apartment for the Captain to translate, who understood a little English. After he had done it, the Commander desired I would walk in and bring my interpreter to peruse and correct it; which I did."

Dinwiddie's letter to the French commander read in part as follows:

Sir:
The lands upon the Ohio River in the western parts of the colony of Virginia, are so notoriously known to be the property of the Crown of Great Britain that it is a matter of equal concern and surprise to me, to hear that a body of French forces are erecting fortresses and making settlements upon that river, within H. M.'s Dominions. . . .

Sir, in obedience to my instructions, it becomes my duty to require your peaceable departure; and that you would forbear prosecuting a purpose so interruptive of

the harmony and good understanding, which His Majesty
is desirous to continue and cultivate with the most
Christian King [Louis XV of France].

Washington requested an early answer to the letter, and St.
Pierre replied that he would hold a council with his officers to consider their reply.

The next day, "The chief Officers retired to hold a Council of
War;" as Washington described it, "which gave me an Oppor-
tunity of taking the Dimensions of the Fort, and making what
Observations I could.

"It is situated on the South, or West Fork of French creek,
near the Water; and is almost surrounded by the Creek, and a
small Branch of it which forms a Kind of Island. Four Houses
compose the Sides. The Bastions are made of Piles driven into
the Ground, standing more than 12 feet above it, and sharp at
Top: With Port-Holes cut for Cannon, and Loop-Holes for the
small Arms to fire through. There are eight 6 lb. pieces
mounted, in each bastion; and one Piece of four Pounds before
the Gate. In the Bastions are a Guard-House, Chapel, Doctor's
Lodging, and the Commander's private Store: . . . There are
several Barracks without the Fort, for the Soldiers' Dwelling;
covered, some with Bark, and some with Boards, made chiefly
of loggs. There are also several other Houses, such as Stables,
Smith's Shop, &c.

"I could get no certain account of the Number of Men here:
But according to the best Judgement I could form, there are an
Hundred, exclusive of Officers, of which there are many. I also gave
Orders to the People who were with me, to take an exact Account
of the Canoes which were hauled-up to convey their Forces down
in the Spring. This they did, and told 50 of Birch Bark, and 170 of
Pine; besides many others which were blocked-out, in Readiness

to make." In assembling this detailed information, Washington had made the best possible use of all the free time the French had given him.

Because of the increasing snowfall and cold, and lack of suitable food, the colonial party's pack and riding horses were becoming weaker day by day. Concerned by their condition, Washington sent them off to Venango, unloaded, under the supervision of Barnaby Currin and two of the other camp attendants. The French had evidently assured him that they would provide canoes to carry the colonial party downstream on its return trip to Venango.

The Half-King had pressed for an audience with the French commandant so he could return the treaty belt, but St. Pierre had so far refused to see him, although he was doing everything in his power to win the Indians over to the side of the French. Finally on December 14 he did meet with the Half-King, but refused to accept the belt. That evening he gave Washington his formal written answer to Governor Dinwiddie's letter.

St. Pierre stated that he would forward the letter to the Marquis Duquesne, Governor of New France, in Quebec, but that French rights to the lands along the Ohio were incontestable. Further, "As to the summons you send me to retire, I do not think myself obliged to obey it. Whatever may be your instructions, mine bring me here by my general's order; and I entreat you, Sir, be assured that I shall attempt to follow them with all the exactness and determination which can be expected from a good officer."

With St. Pierre's response in hand, Washington was eager to head back to Williamsburg as quickly as possible to deliver it to Governor Dinwiddie. Time was of the essence. He realized, however, that the French were using every wile to win the Half-King and his companions to their side, hoping the Indians would stay when Washington left.

The next day the commandant had two canoes filled with liquor and provisions for the party's use as they headed down French Creek to Venango.

But at the same time he was doing everything he could to prevent the Indians from leaving with Washington. "I can't say that ever in my Life I suffered so much Anxiety as I did in this Affair," the young Virginian wrote in his journal.

When Washington pressed the Half-King to leave that day, the Indian leader was unwilling. The French, he told the major, had offered gifts of guns and supplies to the Indians, but these gifts wouldn't be available until the next morning. Washington angrily reminded the Half-King of his treaty obligations to the English, and then confronted the French officers about their delaying tactics. He flatly refused to leave without the Indians.

As a result, the French did give the promised gifts to the Indians the next day, but wanted to seal the bargain with liquor. Knowing this could lead to another delay, Washington spoke heatedly to the Half-King and his companions, saying that they must leave immediately. Surprised by his forceful manner, the Half-King agreed, and the Indians set out with the colonials, the Indians in one canoe, Washington and the others in a second one.

6.

Two Narrow Escapes

We were jammed in the Ice, in such a Manner
that we expected every moment our Raft to
sink, and ourselves to perish.

— GEORGE WASHINGTON
Journal

"We had a tedious and very fatiguing Passage
down the Creek," Washington noted in his journal. "Several Times we were like to have been staved against
Rocks; and many Times we were obliged all Hands to
get out and remain in the Water Half an Hour or more,
getting over the Shoals."

The Half-King and his Indian companions had
gone ahead of Washington and his party, and their canoe
was soon out of sight. The colonials did not catch up
with them until the next day, when they found them
camped beside the creek. They had killed three bears
and were roasting great chunks of meat and gorging
themselves with it. The next day they were unwilling to
go on until they had eaten all the meat they couldn't

carry. Choosing not to wait for them, the colonials went on. The creek was beginning to freeze, and Washington wanted to get to Venango as quickly as possible.

Christopher Gist was also keeping a journal and, three days later, he noted that "The ice was so hard we could not break our way through, but were obliged to haul our vessels across a point of land and put them in the creek again. The Indians and three French canoes overtook us there, and the people of one French canoe that was lost, with her cargo of powder and lead. This night we encamped about twenty miles above Venango."

The next day, December 22, Gist observed that "The creek began to be very low, and we were forced to get out to keep our canoe from oversetting several times; the water freezing to our clothes; and we had the pleasure of seeing the French overset, and the brandy and wine floating in the creek, and [we] run by them, and left them to shift for themselves. Came to Venango, and met with our people and horses."

After spending less than a day at Venango, the colonials started off, leaving their Indian friends behind. The Half-King had told Washington that White Thunder was sick and unable to walk, so they would stay at Venango for several days and then proceed by canoe.

The horses were so weak by this time that they made only five miles the first day, with most of the party walking instead of riding. The next day was very cold, with heavy snow. Washington ordered that everyone except the drivers give up riding, and divide all the baggage and supplies among the exhausted horses. But it wasn't enough. Washington noted, "The Horses grew less able to travel every Day; the Cold increased very fast; and the Roads were becoming much worse by the deep Snow, continually freezing; Therefore . . . I determined to prosecute my journey, the nearest Way through the Woods, on Foot."

To prepare for the ordeal, he changed into Indian dress, with leather leggings and a long coat belted at the waist. "Then," as he recorded, "with Gun in Hand, and Pack on my Back, in which were my Papers and Provisions, I set out with Mr. Gist, fitted in the same manner, on Wednesday the 26th."

Leaving van Braam in charge of the horses and baggage behind them, they traveled eighteen miles on foot that day, and spent the night in an abandoned Indian cabin. The next day they reached Murthering Town. "Here," Gist noted in his diary, "we met with an Indian, whom I thought I had seen at Joncaire's, at Venango, when on our journey up to the French fort. This fellow called me by my Indian name [Annosannoah], and pretended to be glad to see me."

Since Washington wanted to get to the Forks as soon as possible, they asked the Indian to go with them and show them the best way. "We travelled very brisk for eight or ten miles," Gist recorded, "when the Major's feet grew very sore, and he very weary, and the Indian steered too much northeastwardly."

By this time, both Gist and Washington had become mistrustful of their guide's motives. They thought he was trying to lead them astray. Noting that Washington was tired, the Indian offered to carry his gun, which offer was firmly refused. After that, the man grew churlish and sullen. Gist and Washington said that they would stop at the next water. "But before we came to water," Gist noted, "we came to a clear meadow; it was very light, and snow on the ground. The Indian made a stop, turned about; the Major saw him point his gun toward us and fire. Said the Major, 'Are you shot?' 'No,' said I. Upon which the Indian run forward to a big standing white oak, and to loading his gun; but we were soon with him. I would have killed him, but the Major would not suffer me to kill him. . . . [After that] the Major or I always stood by the guns; we made him make a little fire for us by a little run [stream], as if we intended to sleep there. I said to the Major, 'As you will not have him killed, we must get him away, and then we must travel all night.'"

Near sunset they released the Indian, telling him to go on to his cabin. Gist followed him for a short time to make sure he was well out of their way. Then he and Washington traveled all night and most of the next day. At nightfall they spotted Indian tracks, and, wrote Gist, "We parted and appointed a place a distance off, where to meet, it being then dark. We encamped and thought ourselves safe enough to sleep."

Setting out the next morning, the two men reached the Allegheny River. They had thought to cross over the river on the ice, but found that although the ice rimmed the shores out for fifty feet or more, there was then open water in midstream. With one small hatchet their only tool, they spent most of the day building a crude log raft, finishing about sunset.

"This was a whole Day's Work," Washington later noted in his journal. After getting it launched, they set off. "But before we were Half Way over, we were jammed in the Ice, in such a Manner, that we expected every Moment our Raft to sink, and ourselves to perish. I put-out my setting Pole to try to stop the Raft, that the Ice might pass by; when the Rapidity of the Stream threw it with so much Violence against the Pole, that it jerked me out into ten Feet Water: but I fortunately saved myself by catching hold of one of the Raft Logs. Notwithstanding all our efforts, we could not get the Raft to either Shore; but were obliged, as we were near an Island, to quit our raft and Make to it.

"The cold was so extremely severe, that Mr. Gist had all his Fingers, and some of his Toes frozen. . . ." Their sopping wet clothing quickly froze stiff, and they suffered through a miserable night. In the morning, however, the river was frozen solid, and

Returning from their visit to the French at Fort Le Boeuf, Washington and his guide, Christopher Gist, try to cross the ice-clogged Allegheny River on a log raft. *Courtesy of the Library of Congress*

they were able to cross over to the opposite shore and head to John Frazier's cabin, two miles away.

As they waited for their horses to be brought there, Washington visited "Queen" Aliquippa of the Delawares, who resided several miles away. "I made her a present of a Matchcoat and a Bottle of Rum," Washington wrote, "which latter was thought much the better Present of the Two."

Leaving Frazier's cabin on New Year's Day, they traveled on to Christopher Gist's new outpost on the Monongahela, where Washington bought a horse and saddle. Heading back to

Williamsburg several days later, he met a caravan of seventeen horses carrying materials and supplies destined for the British, and the Ohio Company's stronghouse or fort that was to be built at the Forks of the Ohio. The day after that the young major passed a number of families going out to settle. The long-laid plans of the Ohio Company were beginning to be realized.

The summer before, as Washington knew, Governor Dinwiddie had commissioned William Trent, Thomas Cresap, and Christopher Gist—all experienced frontiersmen—to find the best place to build a fortified stronghouse at the Forks and then to build it. Trent was commissioned a captain in the Virginia militia and ordered to raise a company that would help build and garrison the fort. Long suspicious of French designs on the Ohio lands, Dinwiddie wanted to stake out British claims to the area before the French could occupy it. Sending Washington to warn them off was a key part of his plan.

Washington finally reached Williamsburg on January 11, and delivered the letter of the French commander—miraculously safeguarded from the rain and snow and icy waters of the Allegheny— to Governor Dinwiddie. He had been gone seventy-three days, and had traveled in bitter weather through 800 miles or more of snow-covered wilderness.

7.

The French Capture the Forks

If you do not come to our assistance now,
we are entirely undone, and I think
we shall not meet again.

—THE HALF-KING
A message to the colonial governor

Governor Dinwiddie listened to Washington's account of his journey to Fort Le Boeuf with great interest. After reading Commander St. Pierre's reply to his letter—an insolent and defiant response, in his opinion—the Virginia governor realized that the French threat to take over the Ohio country was very real. Immediate steps needed to be taken to stop them!

Swinging into action, Dinwiddie ordered Washington to transcribe the account of his journey from the rough notes he had taken, making them ready for transmission to the King's Council and for immediate publication. He made sure that the published journal was sent to all the colonial governors, and to his British Majesty's court in London, as well. His ardent hope was

37

THE

J O U R N A L

O F

Major *George Washington,*

SENT BY THE

Hon. *ROBERT DINWIDDIE,* Efq;
His Majefty's Lieutenant-Governor, and
Commander in Chief of *VIRGINIA,*

TO THE

COMMANDANT

OF THE

FRENCH FORCES

ON

O H I O.

To WHICH ARE ADDED, THE

GOVERNOR's LETTER;

AND A TRANSLATION OF THE

FRENCH OFFICER's ANSWER.

WILLIAMSBURG:

Printed by WILLIAM HUNTER. 1754

The title page of Washington's journal of his expedition to the French, published in 1754 by Governor Dinwiddie. *Courtesy of the Colonial Williamsburg Foundation*

that Washington's account would make the British and colonial governments recognize the need for immediate action to counteract the French challenge to their interests in the New World.

When he called for help from neighboring colonies, however, Dinwiddie met with little success. Both the Pennsylvania and New York legislatures expressed doubts that the French were actually in British territory. Connecticut, New Jersey, and Maryland all refused funds for defense, and even Dinwiddie's Virginia Assembly was sluggish in providing all the aid Dinwiddie thought necessary. The thirteen colonies simply could not agree on a united course of action. Noting the disarray of the colonies, Benjamin Franklin of Pennsylvania published his famous cartoon of a snake cut into thirteen pieces, with the legend, "Join or Die."

In desperation, Dinwiddie decided to raise a force of 200 militia to send to the Forks as soon as possible to support the men already there building a fort. Just a few days after Washington had returned from Fort Le Boeuf, the governor authorized him to enlist 100 new militiamen from his northern district; and Captain William Trent, at the Forks, was to enlist another 100 men by spring.

Washington would have liked the command of the combined Virginia militia, but wrote to a member of the governor's Council, "I must be impartial enough to confess, it is a charge too great for my youth and inexperience to be entrusted with." It was one of the few times that the future father of his country did acknowledge his lack of experience in such matters.

The man Dinwiddie appointed to command all the forces was the portly, middle-aged Joshua Fry, whose sole qualification seemed to be that he taught mathematics at The College of William and Mary in Williamsburg. Major Washington, promoted to lieutenant colonel, was appointed second in command.

In January 1754, Captain Trent had built a temporary storehouse on the Monongahela to be used as a supply base. In February he and forty militiamen moved to the Forks of the Ohio and began a fortified stronghouse there, constructed of square logs,

with loopholes for musketry. Trent christened the modest structure Fort Prince George, in honor of the Prince of Wales, the
future King George III.

By April the fort was almost finished. The garrison was in
desperate need of food and additional supplies, however, and Trent
left for Wills Creek to try to get what was needed, leaving Ensign
Edward Ward in charge.

In Alexandria, Lieutenant-Colonel Washington was doing his
best to enlist the additional militia that Dinwiddie had ordered, but
was finding it difficult to get the number called for. On March 15
he received new orders from Dinwiddie, instructing him to march
to the Forks with the soldiers he had in order to reinforce Captain
Trent and his men at Fort Prince George. Trent had reported to
the governor that friendly Indians, including the Half-King and his
followers, had warned him that a large French force was on its way
down the Allegheny to oust them.

"You are to act on the defensive," Dinwiddie instructed Washington, "but in case any attempts are made to obstruct the works or
interrupt our settlements by any persons whatsoever, you are to
restrain all such offenders and in case of resistance to make prisoners of, or kill and destroy them!"

"Every Thing being ready," Washington recorded in his diary,
"we began our march according to our orders, the 2nd of April,
with two companies of foot, commanded by Captain Peter Hog
and Lieutenant Jacob Van Braam, five subalterns, two Sergeants,
six Corporals, one Drummer, and one hundred and twenty
Soldiers, one Surgeon, one Swedish Gentleman, who was a volunteer, two wagons guarded by one Lieutenant, Sergeant, Corporal,
and twenty-five Soldiers."

The party traveled very slowly, for the men had to chop down
trees and clear and widen the path through the forest so that the

artillery and vehicles could forge ahead. They were advancing only two or three miles a day, much to Washington's frustration.

Impatient at the slow progress, Washington rode on ahead to scout the land. On April 22 he met a garrison of thirty-three men led by Ensign Ward, second in command of the Forks garrison. The story he told Washington was a sad one.

William Trent, commander at the Forks, had gone east of the mountains on April 13 for much-needed supplies, leaving Ward in charge. The small and rather crude English fort was nearly finished when the garrison saw a fleet of some sixty cargo boats and three hundred canoes coming down the Allegheny carrying "more than a thousand French," Ward declared, with eighteen pieces of artillery.

The French commander, Captain Contrecouer, had demanded immediate surrender, but told Ensign Ward that he would allow the pitiful small English garrison to leave with honor. Faced with this overwhelming French force, Ensign Ward surrendered. The French commander magnanimously fed the colonials dinner and allowed them to leave the next morning. After all, France and England were still formally at peace.

The Half-King had been at the Forks with the British, and had hurled defiance at the French as they took over. He had also sent two warriors with Ensign Ward to find out if English reinforcements were on the way. The Indians were ready to fight the French, he said, "waiting only for your assistance. . . . If you do not come to our assistance now, we are entirely undone, and I think we shall not meet again."

Washington held a council of war after receiving this news, and decided, perhaps foolhardily, considering the few men and supplies he had, to proceed on to Redstone Creek on the Monongahela, some thirty-seven miles from the Forks. The Ohio

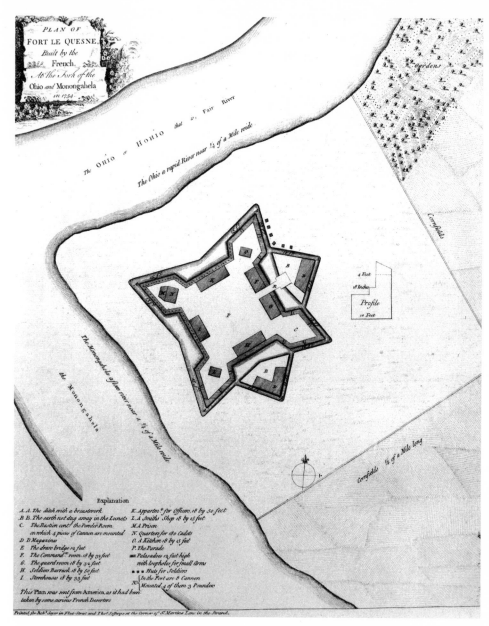

PLAN OF
FORT LE QUESNE.
Built by the
French.
At the Fork of the
Ohio and Monongahela
in 1754

The OHIO or HOHIO that is Fair River

The Ohio a rapid River near ¼ of a Mile wide

Gardens

Cornfields

4 Feet
18 Inches
Profile
10 Feet

The Monongahela a slow river near a ¼ of a Mile wide

the Monongahela

Cornfields ¼ of a Mile long

Explanation

A.A. The ditch with a breastwork.
B.B. The earth not dug away in the Lunets
C. The Bastion cont.s the Powder Room
   on which 4 pieces of Cannon are mounted
D. D. Magazines
E. The draw bridge 12 feet
F. The Command.nt room 18 by 33 feet
G. The guard room 18 by 33 feet
H. Soldiers Barrack 18 by 56 feet
I. Storehouses 18 by 33 feet

K. Appartm.ts for Officers 18 by 50 feet
L. A Smiths Shop 18 by 15 feet
M. A Prison
N. Quarters for 180 Cadets
O. A Kitchen 18 by 15 feet
P. The Parade
▬ Palisadoes 12 feet high
   with loopholes for small Arms
▪ ▪ ▪ Huts for Soldiers
   In the Fort are 8 Cannon
   ✕. Mounted 4 of them 3 Pounders

This Plan was sent from America, as it had been
taken by some curious French Deserters

Printed for Rob.t Sayer in Fleet Street and Thos Jefferys at the Corner of S.t Martins Lane in the Strand.

This plan of Fort Duquesne is based on a diagram drawn in 1754 by Virginia captain Robert Strobo, a prisoner of the French at the fort. The drawing was smuggled out and delivered to the English military forces to use in their campaign against the French. *Courtesy of Clements Library, University of Michigan*

Company had a small storehouse there, and perhaps it could be fortified against the French.

He sent one of the two warriors back to the Half-King, with his answer to the plea for help. "This young man will inform you where he found a small part of our army, making towards you, clearing the roads for a great number of our warriors, who are ready to follow us, with our great guns, our ammunition, and provisions. . . . The other young man I have sent to the Governor of Virginia, to deliver him your speech and your wampum, and to be eyewitness of the preparations we are making, to come in all haste to assist you, whose interest is as dear to us as our lives."

Washington then led the forces onward, as slowly as ever because of the road-building, but was stopped at the Youghiogheny, now in full flood, some twenty miles from Redstone. Food, other supplies, and reinforcements were all desperately needed, but very little of any of them were coming their way. Washington vented his frustration in his correspondence to Dinwiddie. He also fumed with indignation because his pay, and that of the other Virginia officers, was less than that received by officers in the British regular army. To add to his dissatisfaction, messengers arrived with the news that the French were building an imposing fortress at the Forks of the Ohio—Fort Duquesne, named for the governor of New France. Dinwiddie finally wrote to Washington, assuring him that Colonel Fry was coming with reinforcements.

The Youghiogheny flood waters subsided eventually, and Washington did not wait for the promised reinforcements. He and his force were able to cross over and advance slowly over Laurel Ridge and into the Great Meadows beyond. This place, he decided, was an ideal spot to make a defensive stand against the French. "By cleaning the bushes out of these meadows," he wrote, he would prepare "a charming field for an encounter."

Christopher Gist arrived at Washington's camp on May 27 with the news that a party of fifty Frenchmen had passed his nearby house the day before. Hearing this report, Washington sent out a force of seventy-five men under Captain Hog to try to locate them. What they were to do if they found them, he left unclear. An Indian messenger appeared while the party was out, reporting that the Half-King was camped about six miles away, and that the Indian leader had found "the tracks of two men, which he had followed till he was brought thereby to a low obscure place; that he was of the opinion the whole party of French was hidden there."

Leaving half of his men behind, Washington set out with the others, the Indian messenger guiding the way, "in a heavy rain, and in a night as dark as pitch, along a path scarce broad enough for one man; we were sometimes fifteen or twenty minutes out of the path before we could come to it again, and would often strike against each other in the darkness. All night long we continued our route, and the 28th, about sunrise, we arrived at the Indian camp."

The Half-King had about a dozen warriors with him, and after a hasty conference, the Virginians and the Indians agreed to attack the French together. Washington seems to have forgotten Dinwiddie's order "to act on the defensive." His enthusiasm was all for an attack, with no thought that the two colonial powers were nominally at peace with one another.

They promptly set out in the dim light of early dawn, the colonials following the Indians, to the spot where the Half-King had found tracks. Advance scouts soon returned with the report that they had found the French party, some thirty men, "ab't half mile from the Road, in a very obscure place surrounded by rocks."

Seizing the opportunity for a surprise attack, the Indian and colonial forces quickly advanced. Washington's men would be divided, one group coming on the French from the right, the other from the left. The Indians would make up the rear. The enemy would be surrounded.

Washington led the column on the right, and soon came to the edge of the hollow where the French were encamped.

8.

Shots That Set the World on Fire

I heard the bullets whistle, and believe me,
there is something charming in the sound.
— GEORGE WASHINGTON
Letter to his brother Jack

The Virginians had stumbled upon the French sooner than expected, and for a moment they were almost as surprised as the French. Through the early morning mists Washington looked down upon the French camp. A few men were preparing breakfast, others were just rising from sleep and coming out of the bark shelters they had put up as protection from the rain. Suddenly one of the Frenchmen spotted the group above him. He gave a shout of warning and the others began to run for their muskets. Someone fired a shot.

The element of surprise was gone. Washington could not tell whether his other column and the Indian forces were in place, but he saw no reason to delay. He gave his men the order to fire. A volley of shots rang out, and he saw some of the French soldiers fall. He quickly ordered another volley in answer to the scattered fire from the men below.

The bewildered French troops were shouting at one another and running in all directions. Trying to retreat, they found their escape route shut off by the Indians to the rear and the other column of Virginians under Captain Hog. The action was all over in less than a quarter of an hour. Surrendering, the French soldiers flung down their muskets and loudly proclaimed their peaceful intentions.

Their leader, thirty-five-year-old Ensign Joseph Coulon, Sieur de Jumonville, lay wounded on the ground. As Washington stepped forward to accept the surrender, Jumonville proclaimed his party's peaceful intent. The French had come, he said, only to warn the British to leave the territory. That was all. He had a letter that would make this clear, and his interpreter would read it to Washington, which he did.

At the same time, the defeated and defenseless French soldiers were pleading for protection from the Indians, who were coming up from the rear. Washington assured them that they would be safe, but then retired a short distance to have his own interpreter go over the words of the paper Jumonville had given him. While he was preoccupied, the Half-King and his warriors swiftly moved in on the wounded and dead and began killing and scalping them—Jumonville included.

Writing of the event in his diary later, Washington spoke of the main events of the fight in unemotional and very abbreviated form. "We prepared to surround them, marching one after the other Indian fashion: We had advanced pretty near to them, as we thought, when they discovered us; I ordered my company to fire; my fire was supported by that of Mr. Waggoner, and my company and his received the whole fire of the French, during the greater part of the action, which only lasted a quarter of an Hour, before the enemy were routed.

"We killed Mr. de Jumonville, the Commander of the party, as also nine others; we wounded one, and made twenty-one prisoners, among whom were M. la Force, M. Drouillon, and two Cadets. The Indians scalped the dead, and took away the great part of their arms, after which we marched on with the prisoners under guard to the Indian camp."

He did give a little more information in a letter to Governor Dinwiddie, saying, "There were 5 or 6 Indians, who served to knock the poor, unhappy wounded on the head, and bereav'd them of their scalps." As for the surviving French soldiers, now prisoners, Washington was convinced, in spite of Jumonville's letter, that they had come as spies, and not, as they claimed, peaceful ambassadors.

Several days later, encamped at the Great Meadow, he wrote to his younger brother Jack about the affair. In his letter, Washington reported enthusiastically that "I heard the bullets whistle, and, believe me, there is something charming in the sound." Washington had been eager for battle, and utterly fearless in the face of danger.

But in this encounter—the first shots fired in what would develop into a seven-year war, fought mainly in North America but also in Europe, Asia, and the Caribbean—Washington steadfastly refused to acknowledge that he had failed to keep the Indians from massacring a number of wounded and unarmed Frenchmen who had already surrendered.

As future events made clear, Commander Contrecouer and the French at the Forks considered the affair a massacre of defenseless men sent on a peaceful mission to warn the British out of French territory. After all, Washington had visited the French at Fort Le

Boeuf some months before with a similar letter of warning, and the French had treated him with every courtesy.

Contrecouer's view of the whole skirmish as a despicable massacre of innocent men was reinforced by the account of the battle he received from one Denis Kaninguen, whom he described as a deserter "from the English army camp," but who was probably one of the Indian warriors with the Half-King's party. Arriving at Fort Duquesne shortly after the encounter, Kaninguen told Contrecouer that the colonials had made a surprise attack on the peaceful French. When they surrendered, with their leader lying wounded, the Half-King had approached Jumonville and said, *"Tu n'es pas encore mort, mon père."* ("You are not yet dead, my father.") Then the Seneca chief had raised his hatchet and struck the defenseless Frenchman several blows, killing him.

Another account, this time by Private Jim Shaw, a twenty-year-old Irishman from Washington's regiment, also pointed to the Half-King as the murderer of Jumonville. Shaw had not been with the detachment on the morning of the battle, May 28, but he had heard detailed accounts of it from some of the soldiers who had been present. On August 21, he made a sworn statement about this before the governor of South Carolina, where he was then stationed. Part of his account, written down by a scribe as he told it, follows:

> Washington with his Men and the Indians first came upon them [the French] and found them encamped between two Hills. [It] being early in the morning some of them were asleep and some eating, but having heard a Noise they were immediately in great Confusion and betook themselves to their Arms and as this Deponent [a person who testifies under oath] has heard, one of [the

French] fired a gun upon which Col. Washington gave the Word for all his Men to fire. Several of them being killed, the rest betook themselves to flight, but our Indians haveing gone round the French when they saw them immediately fled back to the English and delivered up their Arms desireing Quarter which was accordingly promised them.

Some Time after the Indians came up, the Half-King took his Tomahawk and split the Head of the French Captain having first asked him if he was an Englishman and being told he was a French Man. He then took out his Brains and washed his Hands with them and then scalped him. All this he [Shaw] has heard and never heard it contradicted but knows nothing of it from his own Knowledge only he has seen the Bones of the Frenchmen who were killed in Number about 13 or 14 and the Head of one stuck upon a Stick for none of them were buried, and he has also heard that one of our Men was killed at that Time.

If Jumonville and his party had indeed been on a peaceful mission to warn the Virginians to get out of what the French considered their territory, the French command had good reason to be outraged at this gruesome surprise attack. Ten French soldiers had been killed, and twenty-one taken prisoner. Writing to Governor Dinwiddie, Washington observed that "in strict justice, they ought to be hanged as spies of the worst sort."

Washington was convinced that the French had come with hostile intent. Otherwise, he wondered, why had they not approached openly, with only a small party, to deliver their letter just as he had approached Venango and Fort Le Boeuf some months before? The young Virginian was unwilling to admit, even to himself, that he had managed the affair badly, and had failed to prevent the Indians from slaughtering the Frenchmen.

Governor Dinwiddie, in reporting to his government in London, gave the affair a subtle new twist by writing that "this little skirmish was by the Half-King and the Indians. We were auxiliaries to them, as my order to the commander of our forces was to be on the defensive."

"This little skirmish" was viewed somewhat differently by Horace Walpole, a prominent British man of letters. "The volley fired by a young Virginian in the backwoods of America," he declared, "set the world on fire."

9

Fort Necessity

We have just finished a small palisado'd Fort,
in which, with my small numbers, I shall
not fear the attack of 500 men.

— GEORGE WASHINGTON
Letter to Governor Dinwiddie

Returning to the Great Meadows after the brief battle, Washington that same day wrote in his diary his careful, bare-bones account of what had happened. The next day he used almost the same words to describe the action in a long, rambling letter to Governor Dinwiddie—a letter that began with a lengthy discussion of the meager pay allotted to colonial militia officers as compared to that received by regular British officers of the same rank, and the injustice of it all. Then, after describing the Jumonville skirmish, he told the governor that the strong French forces at Fort Duquesne were sure to mount a retaliatory attack against him. "I shall expect every hour to be attack'd, and by unequal numbers, which I must withstand if there are 5 to 1, or else I fear the Consequence will be we shall loose the Indians, if we suffer ourselves to be drove Back. . . . We have already begun a Palisado'd Fort and hope to have it up tomorrow."

In an earlier passage of the same letter, he had declared that "for my own part I can answer, I have a constitution hardy enough to encounter and undergo the most severe Tryals, and, I flatter myself, resolution to face what any Man durst, as shall be prov'd when it comes to the Test, Which I believe we are upon the Borders off [of]."

Despite this brave talk, Washington's situation was very poor. His little army was ill-equipped, badly clothed, and half-starved. Additional supplies of food, clothing, ammunition, and other necessities were desperately needed. He sent Gist to Virginia with a letter to the governor describing their critical needs.

George Croghan had been appointed the supply contractor for Washington's forces, and he assured the young Virginian that a pack train with 10,000 pounds of flour would be coming by mid-June. Washington was heartened. The Half-King and his company were camped nearby, and Queen Aliquippa had arrived at the Great Meadows with about twenty-five Delaware families—most of them women and children. The Indians consumed great quantities of food every day.

Washington sent the French prisoners under guard to Winchester, and set his men to work reinforcing and finishing his little fort, which he called Fort Necessity. The fortifications were indeed simple: a circular stockade of split logs about seven feet high and fifty feet in diameter, with a small log structure inside in which to store powder and ammunition. Outside the palisade the men dug shallow trenches with earthen embankments to protect them from enemy fire.

The fort was poorly constructed and poorly located—in the middle of a low meadow. There were rising wooded slopes

This reconstruction of Fort Necessity is built on the exact location of the original structure, in Fort Necessity National Battlefield. In the background is a visitor center. The fort,
built in a low meadow surrounded by forested higher land, was a prime target for the
French and Indians. *Courtesy of the author*

beyond, areas in which the enemy could hide and fire down into
the fort. Washington had chosen a bad spot in which to fight. The
Half-King was scornful, calling Fort Necessity that "little thing in
the meadow," but Washington was sublimely confident of its effec-
tiveness. On June 3 he wrote to Dinwiddie: "We have just finished
a small palisado'd Fort, in which, with my small numbers, I shall
not fear the attack of 500 men."

Gist returned on June 6 with the news that Washington's
superior officer, Col. Joshua Fry, had died from injuries received
when he fell from his horse, and that Governor Dinwiddie had
appointed Lieutenant-Colonel Washington to succeed Fry as commander of the Virginia regiment, and commissioned him a full
colonel. Col. James Innes, a friend of the governor, was the newly
appointed commander-in-chief of all the colonial forces.

Washington was gratified at his promotion, but admitted his inexperience in military matters. "I rejoice that I am likely to be happy under the command of an experienced officer and man of sense," he wrote to the governor. "It is ardently what I have wished for." For all that, he didn't want his authority and actions as colonel of the Virginia militia questioned.

Colonel Washington's views and actions were soon challenged, however. In the second week in June three additional companies of his Virginia regiment arrived—180 men—bringing with them nine swivel guns. Three days later, Capt. James Mackay joined him with a company of South Carolina British regulars. Mackay had eighteen years of experience with the British army, and was a veteran of Indian warfare in Georgia. There was immediate friction between him and the young Virginia colonel over the question of command.

Mackay told Washington that since his royal commission outranked colonial ones, he would give the orders in all matters concerning both the colonial and British regular troops. Washington violently disagreed. As a result, the regulars encamped in a separate area from the Virginians, and the two groups had little to do with each other.

Confident that more men and supplies would soon be coming, Washington kept his troops busy building a narrow road to Redstone Creek, about thirty-seven miles from the Forks, where the Ohio Company had a small storehouse. It was back-breaking work—cutting, chopping, dragging wagons and supplies over rocky and heavily forested wilderness. Mackay's regulars were invited to help, but they declined, stating that British regular soldiers did not work on road-building without extra pay, which Mackay had no authority to give.

This enraged Washington, but his men continued the hard work for two weeks through the rough terrain. A number of wagons broke down and many exhausted horses died. Finally they reached Gist's new settlement.

There Washington, Croghan, and the Half-King held a council with the local Indians—Delaware, Shawnee, Mingo, and other nearby tribes. It was soon evident that most of them were switching their allegiance to the French. They were keenly aware of the growing strength of the French at the Forks, and they wanted to side with the winners in this struggle. This was bad news, for these were Indians that the British had counted on for help. The Half-King saw his power eroding too, for the powerful Iroquois federation had proclaimed its neutrality.

One reliable Iroquois chief, Scarroyady, told Washington that the French at the Forks had received massive reinforcements, and would soon be sending a large force—reportedly 800 soldiers and 400 Indians—against the colonials.

Washington's first thought was to reinforce Gist's station, mounting the swivel guns they had brought with them, and await the French. But that plan was soon abandoned. Washington summoned Mackay to a council of war, and they finally decided that it would be best to go back to Fort Necessity and make their stand there. It took several days to return over the half-made road, so many horses having died that the men had to help pull the wagons and guns back themselves.

10.

The French Attack

Our intention has never been to trouble the peace
and good harmony which reigns between two friendly
princes, but only to avenge the assassination
which has been done to one of our officers. . . .

— CAPTAIN COULON DE VILLIERS
Preamble to surrender terms

When they finally reached Fort Necessity on July 1,
the colonial and British forces had only enough meat
and bread for four days, plus about twenty-five cattle,
many of them milk cows. Washington immediately sent
most of his horse teams back to the settlements to
retrieve the needed supplies. The Half-King, disgusted
with the whole set-up, gathered his family and followers
and left. He thought a stand here was hopeless: the fort
was poorly located and hastily constructed, and Washington didn't have enough troops to defend it properly.

On July 2 it rained, and the low meadow became a
bog. Scouts brought word that a large French force was
nearby, and the next morning the enemy appeared at the
edge of the woods. In preparation for the coming battle,

Washington lined up his soldiers outside the earth embankment surrounding the fort, ready to give battle in the open meadow. He hoped that the French would advance in column, as in traditional European warfare. But the French and Indians, experienced in wilderness fighting, did not oblige.

The fort's swivel guns blazed at the enemy. Then, as the French and Indians advanced, the colonial militia leaped behind the embankment for protection, and began firing their muskets. By this time most of the French and Indians had scattered and disappeared among the trees on the wooded slopes around Fort Necessity. From their hiding places they poured a devastating fire down on the British and colonial soldiers, who found little protection in their shallow trenches behind the earthen bulwarks. Many were soon killed or wounded by the relentless enemy attack. Most of the horses and cattle were killed as well. In return, the entrenched soldiers could do little damage to their unseen enemy.

In the late afternoon the rain turned into a heavy downpour, and conditions in Fort Necessity became hopeless. Men crouched in pools of water in the trenches, and powder and muskets were so wet that they would not fire. The casualties continued to mount. As darkness began to fall, the surviving half-drowned soldiers retreated behind the log palisades of the fort. Thoroughly beaten and miserable, fearful that they would soon be killed, some of them broke into kegs holding the fort's rum supply. "It was no sooner dark," wrote Capt. Adam Stephen, one of the company commanders, "than one-half our men got drunk."

Unexpectedly, Washington and his officers heard a voice calling out from the trees where the enemy was. *"Voulez-vous parlez?"* ("Do you want to talk?") Capt. Coulon de Villiers, the leader of the French forces and the older brother of the dead Ensign Jumonville, was offering safe conduct for someone to come and discuss surrender terms.

Washington at first suspected a trick. Why would the French want to talk? They had every advantage. They probably just wanted to find out how bad the conditions were inside the fort. But at last he agreed to send van Braam out under a white flag to talk to them. After a short time, the Dutchman returned with de Villiers' surrender terms, written in French on rain-soaked paper and almost illegible.

The terms seemed almost too good to be true, as van Braam translated them. The colonials and British could march out of Fort Necessity with the honors of war; the prisoners captured in the Jumonville affair were to be returned; and two officers were to remain with the French as hostages.

The surrender was written in French. In English, its preamble stated: "Our intention has never been to trouble the peace and good harmony which reigns between two friendly princes, but only to avenge the assassination which has been done to one of our officers, the bearer of a summons." Later in the document, the word *l'assassin* appeared once again, referring to the Jumonville affair.

In reading the surrender terms in English to Washington, van Braam did not use the words "assassination" or "assassin." He translated the French words as "death" or "killing" as Capt. Adam Stephen and other eyewitnesses later affirmed. In any event, neither Washington or Mackay disputed the translation, and both signed the surrender terms a few minutes before midnight. With a hundred men either dead or wounded, Washington had no other recourse. Van Braam and Robert Stobo, another company commander, volunteered to be the hostages the French demanded.

The next morning, July 4, the defeated army marched out of Fort Necessity, carrying the wounded on litters, or on soldiers' backs, along with their baggage, and with flags flying—the "honors of war." The men were so weary and beaten, however, that they encamped after traveling just three miles. They were too exhausted to go any further. They did not reach Wills Creek until five days later.

Washington hurried on ahead of the troops to get to Williamsburg as quickly as possible to report to Governor Dinwiddie. Meanwhile, the victorious French destroyed Fort Necessity, set fire to Gist's storehouse and to the Ohio Company's storehouse at Redstone Creek. They were intent on wiping out all evidence of English occupation in the Ohio Valley.

In his actions, both in the Jumonville affair and in the fall of Fort Necessity, George Washington had made a number of glaring errors. He had conducted a surprise attack on Jumonville's party in a time of peace between France and Britain; he had failed to prevent the Indians from killing and scalping the wounded soldiers who had surrendered; he had failed with his dealings with the Indians, most of whom were now solidly oriented toward the French; he had built a woefully inadequate defensive fort in the Great Meadows; as a leader he had been unable to keep his soldiers under control during the disastrous battle. And last, but not least, he had unknowingly allowed the French to brand him in the eyes of the world—the French world at least—as an assassin.

11.

Braddock Marches on Fort Duquesne

Instead of pushing on with vigour without regarding
a little rough Road, they were halting to level every
Mole Hill and to erect Bridges over every Brook.

— GEORGE WASHINGTON
Letter to his brother Jack

W hen Washington reached Williamsburg on July
17, he was greeted by most Virginians as a hero who
had fought bravely against overwhelming odds. They
neither believed nor accepted the French accusation,
branding him as an assassin.

In spite of this popular support for Washington, his
resounding defeat at Fort Necessity had not endeared
him to the governor. Dinwiddie now considered him
somewhat of a liability as a military commander. Nevertheless, he ordered the young Virginian to prepare his
regiment and lead it across the Blue Ridge Mountains.
There he was to join Col. James Innes, the recently
appointed commander-in-chief of all Virginia forces.

Together they were to march against the French and oust them from the Forks.

Washington protested that his soldiers were in no condition to march. The battered and beaten regiment had no supplies, little equipment, and no suitable clothes. Many were wounded or sick. Footsore and weary, the men resented such neglect of their needs, and several were deserting every day. Dinwiddie brushed aside Washington's protests, and tartly remarked that any desertions were due to "the want of proper command."

A congress of colonial leaders had been meeting at Albany, New York, during that June and July, with the aim of establishing a colonial union for defense against the French. In spite of a great deal of spirited debate and argument, each colony clung stubbornly to its own priorities. As a result, no unified plan for confronting and defeating the French was made. For the time being, French supremacy in the Ohio country remained unchallenged.

In October, however, Dinwiddie met with the governors of Maryland and North Carolina, and the three of them agreed on a plan—never implemented—to recapture the Forks of the Ohio that fall. Each of the three colonies would contribute troops to make an army of 1,000 men. This would be commanded by Governor Horatio Sharpe of Maryland, who had just been appointed by the British government as commander-in-chief of all provincial forces, even though he had practically no experience as a military man. When Washington heard this news, his heart sank, for Governor Sharpe had publicly criticized the Virginian's behavior and decisions in the Fort Necessity battle.

Washington also learned that, in order to eliminate any dispute between British regular and provincial officers concerning command, his Virginia regiment was to be broken into companies, each of which was to have no higher officer than captain, and all would be commanded by regular army captains. This was too much for Washington. He angrily resigned his commission and left Williamsburg. Governor Sharpe asked him to reconsider, saying that he would see to it that Washington would not be under any officer he would have commanded as a provincial colonel. But George was adamant.

He wrote back to the governor that "if you think me capable of holding a commission that has neither rank nor emolument [financial profit] annexed to it, you must entertain a very contemptible opinion of my weakness, and believe me more empty than the commission itself." He had left the army, he continued, "to obey the call of honor and the advice of my friends, and not to gratify any desire to leave the military line. My inclinations are strongly bent to arms."

Retreating to Mount Vernon, Washington soon settled into the life and routine of a plantation owner. Lawrence's daughter had died, and George was the heir to the estate after the widow, who no longer lived there. He rented it from her for 15,000 pounds of tobacco, to be paid annually. But he enjoyed the rural life only briefly. His longing for a military career was once more aroused when Maj. Gen. Sir Edward Braddock, a friend of King George, arrived at Hampton Roads, Virginia, in February 1755, as the new commander of all British and colonial forces in America. Two regiments of British regulars arrived as well. Braddock had clear orders from the British government: Capture Fort Duquesne.

Sixty years old, Braddock was a career soldier with many years of service with the famous Coldstream Guards, and had experienced a lot of hard fighting in various European wars. He knew all the rules and regulations of the British army and conventional eighteenth-century military strategy and tactics. The army was his life, and as one historian has observed, he was "a bigot to military

rules." Paunchy and hide-bound, Braddock was arrogant and opin-
ionated, and a taskmaster over army discipline. But he was a good
organizer, and energetic. His courage was never doubted.

Soon after the general's arrival, Washington sent him a letter
of congratulation. In doing so, he no doubt wanted to draw atten-
tion to himself, and hoped that the contact might lead to his serving
under Braddock in some way, and perhaps gaining a commission in
the regular army as well.

General Braddock had of course heard of Washington and of
his battle with the French at Fort Necessity. He was also aware
that the young Virginian knew the terrain and difficulties of the
Ohio country much better than most. As a consequence, he
instructed his top aide, Capt. Robert Orme, to write to Washington, stating that the general "will be very glad of your company in
his family [personal staff] by which all inconveniences of that kind
[rank] will be obliviated. I shall think myself happy to form an
acquaintance with a person so universally esteemed."

Braddock had already made it clear to the governors of the
various colonies that he expected that a common defense fund
would be established from all of them, and that the governors
would provide water, supplies, food, and transportation for his
army. In addition, they would supply 3,000 colonial soldiers to fill
up the British regiments.

In mid-April he met again with the colonial governors of New
York, Pennsylvania, Massachusetts, Virginia, and Maryland, and
read them the riot act. He was in a foul mood, lording it over the
governors and treating them like battalion commanders. He had
been promised 299 wagons, 2,500 horses, and supplies for all, he
thundered, but little of any of these had arrived. After this meeting,
the relationship between the general and the colonial officials was
distinctly strained.

Benjamin Franklin's famous cartoon of 1754 urged the colonies to unite against the French enemy, or be defeated. *Courtesy of the Library of Congress*

At Mount Vernon, however, Washington could look down at the Potomac and see British ship after ship arriving from overseas, all of them loaded with military supplies of every sort. He could see that the British were preparing for an all-out effort, and he wanted to be part of it.

Shortly thereafter, he joined the general's staff as a volunteer aide. In this position he hoped once again that he would have the opportunity to be appointed an officer in the regular army, but that was not to be. At the present time, General Braddock explained, he could offer Washington only a temporary commission as a captain. He assured him, however, that after the campaign was over he would use his influences to secure, as Washington put it, "preferment agreeable to my wishes." George

knew that commissions to the regular army were often bought—
the rank of major sold for about £2,000—but he could not
afford that.

Washington got on well with Braddock and the other staff
officers, and tried, as he wrote many years later, to explain to the
general and the other British officers that the Canadian French and
their Indian allies did not fight their battles in the traditional
European manner. "But so prepossessed were they in favor of reg-
ularity and discipline, and in such absolute contempt were these
people [the French and Indians] held, that the admonition was suggested in vain."

These words make the young Washington look good in hind-
sight, but how much he really tried to tell the British officers about
frontier warfare is not known. It is certain that Braddock had only
disdain for the value of Indian allies, and was confident that his
disciplined army could rout the French any time it chose.

In June Braddock gathered his army at Fort Cumberland, now
a strongly fortified structure with stout stockaded walls, cabins, and
storehouses, and defended with artillery. From here the British
engineers began to improve and build the wilderness road to Fort
Duquesne. They were so thorough and exacting—clearing trees,
filling in gullies, bridging every little stream—that they advanced
by only two or three miles daily. At this rate it would be fall before
they reached the French fort at the Forks.

Washington suggested that the army should adapt to wilderness conditions by carrying all supplies on pack horses, and only
the heavy guns should remain on wheels. At first Braddock scorned
this suggestion, but events finally forced him to alter his plans.
American horses were proving too small and weak to pull the heavy
artillery. Soldiers were falling sick with dysentery in the tangled
forests, and the advance was slowing to a creep.

General Braddock's army marches through the Pennsylvania wilderness on its way to the Forks of the Ohio, where the British and colonials planned to take Fort Duquesne and drive the French from the Ohio Valley. *Courtesy of the Library of Congress*

On June 6 Braddock adopted Washington's suggestion. A small army of 1,200 picked troops would dash quickly ahead, with a minimum force of artillery, and all supplies carried on pack horses. The remainder of the army would advance more slowly with the wagons and heavier supplies.

By this time, Washington, too, was ill with dysentery—so weak that Braddock ordered him to stay behind with the rear division. He assured the young Virginian, however, that he could come forward when he felt better, and participate in the attack on Fort Duquesne.

Washington was at first pleased by the reported progress of the advance force, but soon learned, as he wrote to his brother Jack, that "instead of pushing on with vigour without regarding a little rough Road, they were halting to level every Mole Hill and to erect Bridges over every Brook."

After a painful week in the rear, too sick to go on, Washington finally climbed into a cart and was carried by horse to the great crossing of the Youghiogheny. Once there, he again found himself too ill to proceed. He remained there for seventeen miserable days, impatient to join the advance troops, but too weak and helpless to do so.

At last, however, he had improved enough to start out once more, and finally caught up with Braddock and the advance force on July 8. They were encamped just two miles from the Monongahela, and twelve from Fort Duquesne.

Tomorrow, Washington was confident, would see the fort's downfall.

12.

A Disastrous Defeat

> I had 4 Bullets through my Coat, and
> two horses shot under me, and yet
> escaped unhurt.
>
> — GEORGE WASHINGTON
> Letter to his brother Jack

Still weak and sick from his long illness, Washington slept that night in a huge camp organized with military efficiency, with cheery campfires and good food for all. Everyone was confident that the next day would bring them a rousing victory, and the downfall of the French fort.

Early the next morning, Washington rose painfully and prepared to join the general. He hadn't been on his horse for a month, so tied several pillows on his saddle to cushion his seat before riding over to where General Braddock was conferring with his other staff officers.

The military engineers had determined that the army should make two easy crossings of the Monongahela at shallow fords in order to avoid an area of very rough and dangerous country ahead. Washington defined it as an "ugly defile." The advance party under Lt. Col. Thomas Gage had already gone ahead and secured the first crossing. They had seen a few Indians there, who had quickly disappeared. Gage and his men were now securing the second crossing. There the banks were steep, and the engineers were busy cutting them down and smoothing them so that the troops, wagons, and artillery could emerge from the river more easily. The advance parties had noticed a number of Indian tracks in the area and wanted to make sure that the army would be ready for any surprise attack while crossing the river.

Confident in their precautions, the main army made both crossings without incident, and continued its march toward Fort Duquesne, flags and regimental colors proudly waving, and drums beating.

In the lead were the advance scouts, George Croghan and seven Mingo warriors, including the Iroquois chief Scarroyady, who had succeeded the Half-King as the Iroquois delegate to the Ohio tribes after the death of Tanacharisson the previous fall. They were the only Indians with the British. They were followed at some distance by Quartermaster Gen. Sir John St. Clair with 250 engineers and road builders, accompanied by a number of wagons loaded with tools and supplies. On either side were groups of grenadiers, well out on the flanks. Next came General Braddock and his staff and the main body of troops, followed by a long line of wagons loaded with food, ammunition, and supplies, and horses hauling artillery. Behind them were a herd of cattle and a number of camp women who did laundry for the men and, in battle, would help care for the wounded. The rear guard followed, some 200 colonial soldiers. Flankers advanced through the woods on either side of this long military column, a guard against Indians or French.

As they advanced slowly through the relatively open forest on the right bank of the river, a distant shot was heard ahead. A moment later there was a rapid tumult of firing. Had the enemy been sighted? Braddock sent one of his officers galloping ahead to find out what was happening.

Unknown to Braddock and his army, the French commander at Fort Duquesne, Captain Contrecoeur, had decided that his only hope was to try to disrupt the British. If they laid siege to the fort, he knew that heavy artillery would wreak devastation on his defenses; furthermore, his Indian allies would desert him. Indians didn't fight to defend an area. They fought to kill and plunder, to take booty and captives and to win glory for their bravery.

So, on the morning of July 9, Contrecoeur dispatched half his forces at the fort—36 officers, 72 regular soldiers, 146 Canadian militiamen, and more than 600 Indians—to confront the British and ambush them if possible. Capt. Daniel Liénard de Beaujeu, his second in command, led the attack. An inspiring leader, Beaujeu was loved by both the French soldiers and their Indian allies.

It was early afternoon when the opposing parties ran into each other—evidently a surprise to both sides to meet that soon. Groghan and the Mingo scouts spotted the opposing French and Indians first. They hurried back to report their find to Capt. Harry Gordon, one of the road-building engineers who had gone ahead of the others. Looking through the trees, Gordon spotted the French and Indians coming on the run, Captain Beaujeu at their head. At about the same time, the French leader spotted Gordon and the British grenadiers. Taking off his hat, Beaujeu waved it to the left and then to the right, signaling his Indians to separate and envelope the flanks of the approaching army while the French troops attacked the British head-on.

"Braddock's Defeat," July 9, 1755, also known as "The Battle of Monongahela," as depicted by painter Edwin W. Deming. Concealed by rocks and trees in the woodlands, the Indians and French fire at the hapless British and

colonial forces, jammed together on the narrow road. Shot in the chest, General Braddock falls from his mount. *Courtesy of the State Historical Society of Wisconsin (X3)29984*

Alerted, the British grenadiers hurried forward and fired several swift volleys at the enemy. As luck would have it, one chance ball killed Captain Beaujeu.

For a moment the French and Indian forces faltered, but their second in command, Capt. Jean-Daniel Dumas, quickly took over, rallying them and encouraging them to attack. The French and Indians quickly fanned out, scattering and concealing themselves in the forest on either side of the advancing British and colonial forces and firing at them with deadly effect.

Confused by an enemy they couldn't see, and encountering a heavy fire from both sides, Gage's advance troops began a disorganized retreat. Running back, they soon collided with the road builders coming up behind them. Braddock's once orderly advance quickly disintegrated into a scene of utter chaos.

Riding forward, Braddock and his officers tried to stop the retreat, shouting out a confusion of commands to the panicky troops, ordering them to halt, form lines of fire, and attack. But their efforts, Washington later reported, met "with as much success as if we had attempted to have stopped the wild bears of the mountains." Braddock was ordering his soldiers forward by platoons, the traditional European way of fighting. But that style of advance was hopelessly ill-suited to the forest wilderness, against a hidden enemy that was scattered and fighting from cover.

As Washington tried to restore order, his horse was shot from under him. He jumped clear and quickly scrambled onto another mount nearby. Braddock's horse fell too, but the general also got into another saddle and rode through the disorganized troops, shouting orders and trying to muster the men.

The sounds of the rifles were punctuated by the wild cries of the Indians and agonized shrieks of the wounded. Some of the colonial soldiers, more accustomed to wilderness and Indian fighting, took cover as their enemy was doing. As a result, many of them were shot by the British regulars who were still huddled by platoons in the road, and mistook them for the enemy.

Braddock had a second horse shot from under him, but quickly mounted another, and continued his efforts to restore order. Washington offered to muster the colonial soldiers and engage the French and Indians in their own way, but Braddock indignantly refused. He then ordered a charge at some of the enemy that had come into view on the right, but the terrified soldiers hesitated.

To inspire them, Braddock and the other officers rode ahead, leading the charge through the underbrush. The only result was enemy fire that struck Braddock in the chest. He fell, gravely wounded. Two of his aides were wounded as well.

Washington's second horse fell, and a bullet went through his hat. He was able to corral another mount and rode to where several doctors were hovering over the wounded general. Untouched by the bullets that whistled around him, Washington gazed at his stricken leader and felt, as he wrote to his brother Jack several days later, "the miraculous care of Providence that protected me beyond all human expectations; I had 4 Bullets through my Coat, and two horses shot under me, and yet escaped unhurt."

13.

The Long Retreat

We shall know better how to deal
with them another time
— GENERAL BRADDOCK
Shortly before his death

Braddock, lying on the ground severely injured, finally gave Washington permission to have his men fight the enemy in their own way. But it was too late. Painfully ill and weak, Washington later observed that "I was the only person left to distribute the Gen'ls Orders, which I was scarcely able to do, as I was not half over'd from a violent illness." A few minutes later, the general sank into unconsciousness.

By this time, Washington had little hope that an effective stand could be mounted against the enemy by the disorganized surviving troops. He therefore directed that the wounded general be placed in a cart, then accompanied him and the few soldiers that were still around him back across the Monongahela ford. Halting on a slight hillock on the other side, he formed the troops into a defensive position as best he could.

Rousing briefly, General Braddock thought not of himself, but of his army. He told Washington to ride back and find the rear division—some forty miles behind—and have it send provisions forward for his surviving troops, and cover their orderly withdrawal.

As dusk fell, Washington began the long ride to the rear. Although unwounded, he was still pitifully weak, not only because of his long illness but also because of the unbelievable exertions

Mortally wounded, General Braddock is carried from the battlefield in a cart. This engraving was made from an original painting by Alonso Chappel, which belongs to the Chicago Historical Society. *Courtesy of the Library of Congress*

and actions he had endured that fateful day. The cries of the wounded, and the wild warwhoops of the Indians rang in his ears as he swept by them. Many years later he wrote down his recollections of that terrible night ride. "The shocking scenes which presented themselves on this night march are not to be described. The dead—the dying—the groans—lamentations—and crys along the Road of the wounded for help . . . were enough to pierce a heart of adamant. The gloom & horror . . . was not a little encreased by the impervious darkness occasioned by the close shade of thick woods. . . ."

After long hours of riding, Washington finally reached the rear camp the next morning. Here he found the officers and soldiers terrified and disorganized; they were all fearful that the French and Indians would soon be coming to overwhelm them too. Their senior officer, Col. Thomas Dunbar, was in as much of a funk as the rest of them and, for no reason that Washington could see, ordered that the drums beat to arms.

Some provisions were finally sent forward to Braddock, and Washington took to his bed, overcome with fatigue and illness. During the next two days, the survivors of Braddock's command joined them, as well as the gravely wounded general himself, mounted on a horse. He ordered that all stores, mortars and ammunition be destroyed, and the defeated army head back to Fort Cumberland, seventy-five miles away.

General Braddock, a musket ball lodged in his chest, did not live to get there. He died on July 14, a short distance beyond the site of Fort Necessity. Shortly before his death he observed, as if talking to himself, "We shall know better how to deal with them another time." At Washington's direction, he was buried in the middle of the primitive road. Many wagons were driven over the grave to obliterate it so that the Indians would not find and dishonor the body of the fallen British leader.

The battered and thoroughly beaten army—some 2,000 British and colonial troops, perhaps 1,350 of them fit for active duty—reached Fort Cumberland on July 25. It was clear that Colonel Dunbar had no thought of attempting another challenge to the French this year. He and his troops continued on to Philadelphia where they went into "winter quarters" in midsummer.

Two-thirds of Braddock's advance force had either been killed or wounded, while French losses were slight—some twenty-six dead and sixteen wounded. The French Indians had taken many captives, and were rich with scalps and plunder. The decisive defeat of the British insured that almost all of the Ohio Indians were now securely allied with the French. Only the Mohawks were still friendly to the British. The other Iroquois nations struggled to maintain their neutrality.

General Braddock had been a brave and courageous soldier, but he was too much of a spit-and-polish, going-by-the-book officer to adapt successfully to wilderness warfare. He had only contempt for Indians, and would have little to do with even the friendly ones. Chief Scarroyady told the governor and council of Pennsylvania that Braddock "was a bad man when he was alive; he looked upon us as dogs and would never hear anything that was said to him. We often endeavored to advise him of the danger he was in with his Soldiers; but he never appeared pleased with us. . . ."

Washington, however, had little criticism for the general. He blamed the "dastardly behavior of the Regular Troops" for the defeat, and went on to say "how apt are mankind to level their vindictive Censures against the unfortunate Chief, who perhaps merited least of the blame."

14.

Blood and Terror on the Frontier

For the next two years there was hardly,
in the grim parlance of the frontier, "a dry
settlement" along the western border, hardly a
night but what there was "blood on the moon."

— WALTER O'MEARA
Guns at the Forks

From Fort Cumberland, Washington wrote to Governor Dinwiddie on July 18, describing the disastrous defeat: "We were attack'd (very unexpectedly I must own) by abt. 300 French and Ind'ns; Our numbers consisted of abt. 1300 well arm'd Men, chiefly Regular's, who were immediately struck with such a deadly Panick, that nothing but confusion and disobedience of orders prevail'd amongst them: the officer's in gen'l behav'd with incomparable bravery, for which they greatly suffer'd, there being near 50 kill'd and wound'd. . . . The Virginian Companies behav'd like Men and died like Soldiers; . . . the dastardly behavior of the English Soldier's expos'd all those who were inclined to do their duty to almost certain Death."

As disastrous and inexplicable as the defeat at the Forks had been, Colonel Dunbar's decision to retreat with all his forces to Philadelphia and into winter quarters only made the situation worse. The frontiers of Virginia, Pennsylvania, and New York now lay exposed and defenseless to attacks by the victorious French and Indians.

"Dunbar's decision to march to Philadelphia," Governor Sharpe of Maryland wrote to Dinwiddie, "has alarmed the frontier more than Braddock's defeat."

"I must confess that the whole conduct of Colonel Dunbar appears monstrous," Dinwiddie replied. He wrote to Dunbar on July 26, trying to prod him into some military action. "Are you not able, after a proper refreshment of your men, to make a second attempt to recover the loss we have sustained? . . . If you cannot attack the fort in form, you may be able to besiege them, and by preventing any supplies of provisions, starve them out. . . . You must still have remaining upwards of 1600 men, and . . . I think I can promise you a reinforcement of at least 400 men."

Dunbar, however, refused to consider any such action against the enemy. The British and colonial forces has been soundly beaten, and he considered any effort to attack Fort Duquesne this year foolhardy.

The French and Indians, exultant after their unexpected victory on the Monongahela, had returned to Fort Duquesne to celebrate. The Indians were loaded with plunder and scalps, and had a number of captives, some of whom they tortured and burned at the stake. Soon thereafter they scattered to their various villages to recount their victories and show off the booty they had gathered from the fallen enemy.

The French, hardly daring to believe that their spectacular victory had really happened, were at first uncertain as to the intentions of the defeated British. It was soon evident, however, that these forces had no intention of mounting another attack on them in the near future. For the moment, the whole frontier lay exposed and defenseless before them.

Seizing the opportunity, both the French and the Indians began a series of hit-and-run raids against isolated frontier towns and settlements. These attacks were nearly always carried out by small parties, often no more than fifteen or twenty men. Sometimes all the raiders were Indian warriors, bent on killing and scalping as many luckless frontier people as they could. The usual tactic was to pounce on their victims by surprise, kill and destroy, then quickly vanish into the big woods before any resistance could be mounted against them.

Such attacks were usually very successful. "For the next two years," wrote one historian of the period, Walter O'Meara, "there was hardly, in the grim parlance of the frontier, 'a dry settlement' along the western border, hardly a night but what there was 'blood on the moon.'

"In Pennsylvania the storm broke at the little settlement of Penn's Creek, on the Susquehanna. Here, on October 16, the Delaware suddenly swooped down and killed or carried off 25 people. Soon afterwards, the same Indians wiped out 47 families along the Maryland border, and razed 27 plantations."

As such attacks continued, hordes of panic-stricken and defenseless families began to flee eastward from the frontier farms and settlements of Pennsylvania, to seek refuge in larger communities. In Virginia it was the same story, as the raiders struck many areas along the Maryland border, the Shenandoah Valley, and the Blue Ridge Mountains. By summer's end, the war parties had hit isolated spots as far south as the Carolinas.

Realizing the dangers of the exposed frontiers, Governor Dinwiddie commissioned Washington colonel of the Virginia Regiment and commander-in-chief of all Virginia forces. He further instructed him to recruit new members to bring the regiment up to full strength, and to prepare and man a series of frontier forts, or strong houses.

That was more easily ordered than done. The newly promoted commander-in-chief of Virginia forces had little luck recruiting the soldiers needed, or in securing the food, clothing, and other supplies which he deemed vitally necessary for their needs.

Further troubles and discouragement came when Washington proceeded to Fort Cumberland, where members of his regiment who had survived the Braddock debacle were stationed, under the nominal command of Lt. Col. Adam Stephen. A company of thirty Maryland soldiers were there too, led by one Capt. John Dagworthy. There was immediate friction and ill-feeling between Washington and Dagworthy, who had been lording it over Stephen, and now tried to give orders to the Virginia colonel. Because of a paper given to him years before, Dagworthy claimed that he was an officer of the regular British army and, as such, could give orders to any colonial officer, no matter what his rank. Washington was outraged at the very idea, and protested strongly to Governor Dinwiddie.

Besides the constant friction with Dagworthy, Washington found general conditions at the fort deplorable. Discipline was very lax, with soldiers frequently drunk or disorderly, and new draftees sullen and insolent. Necessary supplies that had been ordered either came late or not at all, and the regiment was nowhere near full strength. Washington did everything in his power to reinstate military rules and discipline, but to little avail. He was in despair, and considered resigning.

Spreading terror on the frontier with their French allies, a band of Indians attack a wilderness cabin, setting it on fire and killing the pioneer family. Etching by Harley, in *A New History of the United States*, 1898.

He felt more frustration later, when he toured the frontier settlements. Many farms were deserted because of the frequent Indian raids—their owners having fled east of the mountains to more settled areas. Others who stayed to face the Indian danger had made their cabins or public buildings into private forts or "strong houses" by boarding up windows and making loopholes from which to fire at attackers. The militia, called to help guard the frontier, was proving to be of little use.

Washington hoped—in vain—that the friendly Cherokee and Catawba Indians to the south could be persuaded to come to the aid of the Virginians against the Ohio French-allied Indians. "Indians," he believed, "are the only match for Indians, and without them we shall ever fight upon unequal terms." More than a year later, however, when a sizeable contingent of the southern Indians did come to help the Virginians, Washington changed his tune, for he found them impossible to control. "They are the most insolent, most avaricious and most dissatisfied wretches I have ever had to deal with," he declared.

In spite of all his frustrations and setbacks, he was, as his biographer James Thomas Flexner noted, "enrolled in a school of experience that would in many ways prepare him for the world-shaking task [commander of all American forces in the Revolutionary War] he was to undertake almost twenty years later."

15.

Troubles of Command

It is hard to have my character arraigned,
and my actions condemned, without a hearing.

— GEORGE WASHINGTON
Letter to Governor Dinwiddie

Disheartened by the general chaos at Fort Cumberland and on the frontier, Washington headed for Williamsburg to report to the governor. He complained bitterly about conditions at the fort—especially the difficulty of dealing with Captain Dagworthy—and stressed the need for more recruits, food, and supplies of every kind. When the Virginia Assembly heard about the deplorable conditions at Cumberland and the disorderly behavior of the soldiers, it revised the military law, decreeing death for mutiny, desertion, or disobeying orders.

In early February 1756, with Governor Dinwiddie's permission, the twenty-three-year-old Washington set off to Boston to meet with Governor Shirley of Massachusetts, who had succeeded to command after

Braddock's death. There he hoped to plead his case for being commissioned a regular British officer, and to refute Captain Dagworthy's assumption that he could give orders to a provincial colonel.

After meeting with Washington in early March, Governor
Shirley ruled that Dagworthy could only rank as a provincial captain, and Washington should take command at Fort Cumberland.
The Virginia colonel also learned that Shirley, just a few days
before, had appointed Governor Sharpe of Maryland to command
all the provincial troops raised in Pennsylvania, Maryland, Virginia, and South Carolina, and that a campaign against Fort
Duquesne was being planned.

Back at Williamsburg, Washington wrote to Governor Shirley
requesting a commission as second in command for the Fort
Duquesne campaign. He also sent a copy of this letter to Governor Sharpe, asking his approval. Perhaps to his surprise, Sharpe,
who had publicly criticized Washington's military decisions in the
Fort Necessity battle, did recommend him for the job.

Heading on to Winchester in the Shenandoah Valley, Washington found conditions there very bad, with the local soldiers in
disorganized panic over the continuing Indian raids, some of them
quite nearby. The militia that had been called to service in this
time of crisis was of little or no use. What was needed, Washington believed, was the strengthening of the regular forces—the
Virginia Regiment. On April 24 he wrote a despairing letter to
Governor Dinwiddie: "Honble. Sir: Not an hour, nay scarcely a
minute, passes, that does not produce fresh alarms and melancholy
accounts. . . . Every day we have accounts of such cruelties and
barbarities, as are shocking to human nature."

Three days later he wrote more of the same. "Desolation and
murder still increase, and no prospects of relief. The Blue Ridge is
now our frontier, no men being left in this country, except a few
that keep close with a number of women and children in forts,

which they have erected for that purpose. There are no militia in this country; when there were, they could not be brought to action."

For some time Washington had been urging the building of a strong fort at Winchester as "a place of refuge for the women and children in time of danger." He further recommended that it be the principal Virginia frontier fort instead of Fort Cumberland, which was, after all, in Maryland.

Shortly after receiving his colonel's gloomy messages, Governor Dinwiddie sent him a sharp rejoinder: "I hope the affairs of the regiment are not in so bad a condition as represented here. The Assembly were greatly inflamed, being told that the greatest immoralities and drunkeness have been much countenanced, and proper discipline neglected; I am willing to think better of our officers and therefore suspend my judgement until I hear from you."

Washington was quite self-defensive in his reply: "I have both by threats and persuasive means, endeavored to discountenance gaming, drinking, swearing, and irregularities of every other kind; while I have, on the other hand, practiced every artifice to inspire a laudable emulation in the officers for the service of their country, and to encourage the soldiers in the unerring exercise of their duty. . . . The unhappy difference about the command, which has kept me from Fort Cumberland, has consequently prevented me from *enforcing* the orders, which I never fail to *send*. . . ." Again he considered resigning.

In Washington's view, Dagworthy was the culprit responsible for the breakdown in regimental discipline and behavior. Because of his ongoing conflict with the Maryland captain over who was in charge, Washington had spent little time at Fort Cumberland, and Dagworthy had a free hand in lording it over the Virginia officers and men. As a result, proper military order and discipline had disintegrated.

In June, Governor Shirley was recalled to England, and a regular British army general, John Campbell, Fourth Earl of Loudoun, arrived a month later as the new commander-in-chief of all forces. In his honor, Washington named the fort he was building in Winchester Fort Loudoun.

In spite of Washington's efforts, conditions on the Virginia frontier continued as bad as ever. Small bands of French Indians made frequent raids, leaving death and terror in their wake. The dismal performance of the militia, the citizen army, in protecting the frontier prompted another disconsolate letter to Dinwiddie in November: "For the want of proper laws to govern the militia by (for I cannot ascribe it to any other cause), they are obstinate, self-willed, perverse, of little or no service to the people, and very burdensome to the country.... Concerning the garrisons, I found them very weak for want of men; but more so by indolence and irregularity."

Discouraged almost beyond reason, Washington turned to Lord Loudoun in January 1757, when he wrote his new commander-in-chief a long, rambling, blatantly self-serving letter. In it, he laid the blame for most of the British reverses in the struggle with the French to the ill-considered orders and miscalculations of the Virginia Assembly, and the relative inactivity of the neighboring colonies.

In April 1754, he related, his Virginia soldiers had been forced to march toward the Forks "without tents, without clothes . . . never recovering in all that space [until July, after the battle in the Meadows] any subsistence." The lack of provisions and supplies of every kind had fostered discontent and desertions, he asserted. "How strongly I have urged the Governor and Assembly to pursue different measures. . . . But no regard has hitherto been paid to my remonstrances. . . . My unwearied endeavors are inadequately rewarded. The orders I receive are full of ambiguity. I am left, like a wanderer in the wilderness, to proceed at hazard. I am answerable for consequences, and blamed, without the privilege of defense." He also stated that if General Braddock had lived "I should have met with preferment agreeable to my wishes." The letter ended with fawning reference to General Loudoun's admirable character and his "important services performed to his Majesty in other parts of the world."

Washington's extreme frustration and anger were clearly highlighted in that letter. Granted, he was facing nearly insurmountable difficulties, and believed that he had been unjustly treated. Much of what he said *was* true. Nevertheless, in this intemperate youthful outburst, he came perilously close to disloyalty toward his superiors, if he had not indeed crossed that line.

The next month, with Dinwiddie's reluctant permission, Washington traveled to Philadelphia to present in person his case to Lord Loudoun, who was there for a conference with the provincial governors. It was several weeks before the young Virginian was granted an interview with Loudoun—an interview in which he was sternly rebuffed. There would be no attack on Fort Duquesne that year; Fort Cumberland was to be maintained, but by Maryland troops; 400 Virginia troops were to be sent to South Carolina; and his lordship would not even listen to Washington's arguments about making his Virginia regiment part of the regular British army.

Discouraged, Washington spent much of the summer of 1756 trying to rebuild his regiment, but was almost in despair because of the desertions. To inspire a fear of the consequences, he had a gallows constructed, and finally, on June 28, he reluctantly ordered that two notorious deserters be hung, as an example to others who might consider taking similar leave. His heart wasn't in such punishment, however, for he subsequently pardoned a number of other deserters.

In August he was much disturbed to hear rumors that a Colonel Corbin had maligned him, saying that Washington had made false statements about desperate conditions at the frontier in order to wrest more money from the Assembly. Such reports affected him deeply, for nothing was more important to young Washington than his personal honor. He wrote an indignant letter to Governor Dinwiddie concerning the matter.

"It is uncertain in what light my services have appeared to your Honor; but this I know, and it is the highest consolation I am capable of feeling, that no man, that was ever employed in a public capacity, has endeavored to discharge the trust imposed in him with greater honesty, and with more zeal for the country's interest, than I have done. . . . It is hard to have my character arraigned, and my actions condemned, without a hearing."

Dinwiddie had recently suffered a stroke and had asked for a recall to England. He replied on September 24, a week later: "I would gladly hope there is no truth in it. I never heard of it before . . . I'd advise you not to credit every idle story you hear for if I was to notice reports of different kinds, I should be constantly perplexed. My conduct to you from the beginning was always friendly, but you know I had good reason to suspect you of ingratitude which I am convinced your own conscience and reflection must allow I had reason to be angry, but this I endeavor to forget. . . . I wish my successor may show you as much friendship as I have done."

In reply, Washington wrote: "I do not know, that I ever gave your Honor cause to suspect me of ingratitude, a crime I detest, and would just carefully avoid. If an open, disinterested behavior carries offense, I may have offended. . . . If instances of my ungrateful behavior had been particularized, I would have answered to them. But I have long been convinced, that my actions and their motives have been maliciously aggravated."

Dinwiddie did not respond. His letter of September 24 was almost the governor's last letter to his demanding and often cantankerous youthful commander. Two months later, dispirited and in ill health, he left Virginia for England.

For the past year, the governor's relationship with Washington had been rocky. He had, it is true, often issued orders that were either vague or very hard for Washington to carry out without the necessary follow-through of vitally needed supplies. Nonetheless, he had usually backed his testy commander and done his best to satisfy his wishes.

16

Forbes Road

If Colo. Bouquet succeeds in this point with
the General, all is lost! All is lost by Heavens!
Our Enterprise Ruin'd. . . .

— GEORGE WASHINGTON
Letter to General Forbes's aide

Washington had been plagued all fall with a return
of dysentery—the "bloody flux." Perhaps that explained
some of his recent touchiness and bad humor. In November he became seriously ill, running a fever and suffering repeated sharp pain whenever he breathed deeply.
Dr. James Craik, his army physician at Winchester, bled
him several times, to no avail. Soon he was so weak that
he could barely walk.

Perplexed by Washington's confusing symptoms
and convinced that he was gravely ill, the doctor told
his fellow officers that rest and quiet, and a change of
air offered "the best chance that now remains for his
recovery."

With that discouraging prognosis, Washington turned his command over to his close and trusted friend, Capt. Robert Stewart, and made his painful way back to Mount Vernon. For weeks he was so sick that he sometimes thought he was going to die. Disconsolate, he brooded over his health, his continuing problems on the frontier, and the fact that he had failed in his long struggle to gain a regular British army commission. "I now have no prospect left of preferment in a military way," he noted sadly.

In March he traveled to Williamsburg to consult Dr. John Anson, Virginia's foremost doctor. Much to his surprise and relief, he received a good report. He would live; he was on the road to recovery; he would be all right.

The doctor's cheery diagnosis was just the tonic Washington needed. Within days he was feeling fit, and his thoughts turned once again to the military—and to matrimony! Fully recovered, he set off to call on Martha Custis, whom he had just met, at her White House Plantation on the Pamunkey River. Recently widowed, Martha was a trim and attractive woman of twenty-six, one of the richest unmarried ladies in Virginia.

George called on her several times that month, and they evidently reached an "understanding" before he set off in early April for Winchester to assume his command of the Virginia Regiment. Once there, he found the military situation quite different.

When Washington had left his command the November before, the British and provincials were looking back at three nightmare years—one defeat after another, starting with Washington's surrender at Fort Necessity, then Braddock's disastrous defeat at the Forks of the Ohio, followed by two years of blood and terror on the frontiers. The French general Montcalm had taken Fort

Oswego on Lake Ontario and Fort William Henry on Lake George as well, and General Loudoun had failed miserably in his campaign to capture Louisburg, the French fortress guarding the entrance to the St. Lawrence River. The future for the British cause looked dark.

But great changes were in the works. In June 1757, William Pitt, the earl of Chatham, became secretary of state in London, with full control over England's foreign and military affairs. Called "the Great Commoner" by his admirers, Pitt had entered Parliament in 1735, and gained much influence because of his powerful oratory and knowledge of foreign affairs.

As secretary of state, Pitt was determined to reverse the ill tides of war and bring victory to Britain in America. One of his first acts was to recall Loudoun and replace him as commander-in-chief in America with Gen. James Abercrombie, a close friend of King George II.

Intent on defeating the French in America, Pitt mapped out a grand, three-pronged strategy. Three major campaigns would be undertaken in 1758, all against vital French strongpoints. General Abercrombie would lead an expedition against the French on Lake George. Gen. Jeffery Amherst was to attack and take Louisburg. Finally, Brig. Gen. John Forbes would march on Fort Duquesne.

When Washington returned to duty, the Virginia Assembly had just voted to increase the Virginia forces to 2,000 soldiers in two regiments—the existing one and a new regiment of 1,000 men to be enlisted for a short term of duty, ending on December 1. By that time it was assumed that Fort Duquesne would be taken and the campaign finished.

As Washington struggled to get his regiments ready at Winchester, General Forbes was gathering his forces at Philadelphia and making plans for the advance to the Forks. All in all he would have 1,000 British regular soldiers, 2,700 Pennsylvanians,

1,600 Virginians, and other smaller forces, making a grand total of between 6,000 and 7,000 troops for the march on Duquesne. Much to Washington's satisfaction, Pitt had decreed that "colonial officers should command all regulars of inferior rank."

One decision Forbes had to make was the route he would take to Fort Duquesne. Washington naturally assumed that Braddock's road was the only possible route, for it had been cut and cleared to within a few miles of the fort. The Pennsylvanians, however, had other ideas. The best route, they argued, would be westward from Philadelphia. A new road would have to be cut through the mountains, but it would be better than the path Braddock had taken.

Washington was furious at the idea of a route entirely through Pennsylvania. He was sure that the Braddock road would serve the coming military campaign best. After all, he had helped build much of it and knew its good points. He was convinced that it was the easiest route to the Forks, had fewer mountains in its path, and had closer access to settlements and supplies. Above all, it was *there*, ready to be used. But Washington was also keenly aware that after the war was over, the choice of roads would bring huge commercial advantages to the winner—either Pennsylvania or Virginia. And Washington was a loyal Virginian. The stakes were high, not only for Virginia, but for the Ohio Company as well.

General Forbes was a serious and methodical Scotsman, a career British army officer, well-versed in the military arts. He was determined not to make the mistakes that Braddock had made. His second in command was Swiss-born Col. Henry Bouquet, thirty-nine years old, an experienced veteran who had served in the armies of three other nations before joining the British army. These two officers were seasoned experts of European-style military service, but, unlike Braddock, they were also open to adapting themselves to the special needs of fighting Indian-style in the wilderness.

Forbes had at first evidently favored the Braddock road, but had listened with an open mind to advisers who thought a road entirely through Pennsylvania would be better. Good roads already existed from Philadelphia westward to Harris's Ferry on the Susquehanna, nearly halfway across the colony, and on through Carlisle and Shippensburg.

Washington was so convinced that the Braddock road was best that he wrote letter after letter to Colonel Bouquet, citing all the reasons why he thought it would be disastrous to make a new road. Fearing that Bouquet favored the Pennsylvania route, he sometimes overstepped the bounds of military protocol in his outbursts. Meanwhile, he set to work clearing and widening the Braddock road from Fort Cumberland.

At the same time, General Forbes had his men at work extending the Pennsylvania road westward, and Washington was in despair. In late July he wrote to Bouquet from his camp in Fort Cumberland, trying once again to persuade him that his view was the right one. He started, however, on a conciliatory note:

"I shall most cheerfully proceed on any Road; pursue any Rout; or enter into any Service; that the General or yourself can think me usefully employ'd in; and shall never have a Will of my own, when a duty is required of me: but since you desire me to speak; permit me to observe this that after having convers'd with all the Guides, and been convinced by them and every other who has knowledge of the Country, that a Road comparable to General Braddocks (or indeed fit for any Service at all even for carrying Horses) cannot be made, I own I say after this, I shou'd sollicit that route with less warmth; . . . I should however be extremely glad of one hours conference with you and that when the general arrives, I cou'd then better explain myself."

In reply, Bouquet cautiously observed: "Nothing can be greater than your generous dispositions for the service and the

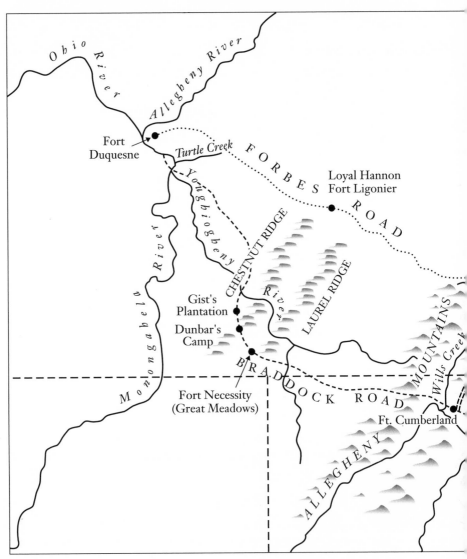

Rival roads to the Forks of the Ohio. The Forbes road through Pennsylvania, which Washington opposed, is depicted in dots. Below it the Braddock road,

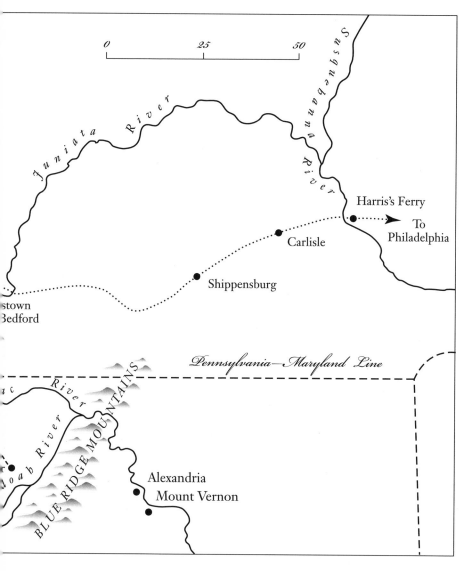

candid Exposition of your Sentiments. . . . Therefore I desire to have an interview with you."

General Forbes, who would have the final say about the road, warmly supported Bouquet's meeting with Washington. Perhaps the Swiss colonel, an experienced conciliator, could smooth out the dispute and placate the Virginian. This Bouquet tried to do, but he could not sway Washington's views. Nor could Washington convince Bouquet that he was right.

Frustrated and angry, Washington went over the head of his superior several days later, and wrote an impassioned letter to his friend, Maj. Francis Halkett, General Forbes's principal aide. He hoped Halkett could convince the general.

"I am just returned from a Conference held with Colo. Bouquet. I find him fix'd, I think I may say fix'd, upon leading you a New way to the Ohio; thro a Road, every Inch of it to [be] cut, at this advanced Season, when we have scarce time left to tread the beaten Tract; universally confess'd to be the best Passage through the Mountains.

"If Colo. Bouquet succeeds in this point with the General, all is lost! All is lost by Heavens! Our Enterprise Ruin'd."

When General Forbes saw this letter he judged it "most impertinent" and wrote to Bouquet that such behavior was "a shame for any officer to be concerned in." Later, in a conference at Raystown, General Forbes dressed down the Virginia colonel and his officers in no uncertain terms for their weakness in declaring "so publicly in favor of one road without knowing anything of the other."

Just as Washington had feared, Forbes and Bouquet had made up their minds. The army would advance through Pennsylvania, building the new road as they went. Part of Forbes's methodical plan was to build forts or supply bases every forty miles or so on the new road, strongholds to fall back upon if necessary.

The decision had been made, but Washington was still unwavering in his opposition. On the first day of September, he wrote his friend John Robinson, Speaker of the Virginia House of Burgesses. His commanders, he declared, "are d—ps [dupes] or something worse to P-S-V-N [Pennsylvania] Artifice. Nothing now but a Miracle can bring this Campaigne to a happy Issue. . . . By the last Accts. I receiv'd they had cut it [the road] to the Foot of Laurel Hill about 35 Miles and I suppose by now 1500 Men have taken post at Loyal hanning about 10 Miles further, where our next Fort is intended to be constructed."

17

Fort Ligonier

[My life was] in as much jeopardy
as it had ever been before or since.

— GEORGE WASHINGTON
Writing many years later of a French
attack near Fort Ligonier

The forces of General Forbes were now gathered at Raystown, some thirty miles north of Fort Cumberland, where a new strongpoint, Fort Bedford, had been constructed. A north-south road was cut connecting the two. Meanwhile, more than a thousand men were clearing the new road over the Allegheny Mountains, and another strongpoint, Loyal Hannon, was being built on the far side of Laurel Ridge. Soon the bulk of the army advanced to this most western fort, which would be called Fort Ligonier.

There, Colonel Bouquet listened to the pleadings of Maj. James Grant of the 77th Regiment of Highlanders for some offensive action. Grant longed for fame and heroic action, and was sure he was the one to carry it off.

Persuaded, on September 9 Bouquet gave Grant permission to lead 850 men on a reconnaisance-in-force against Fort Duquesne. They were to investigate the present state of the fort, its strength, supplies, and the number of French troops and Indians there to defend it. If possible, they were also to capture a few prisoners for questioning back at Loyal Hannon. Bouquet even went so far as to give Grant permission to raid the French fort if conditions were favorable.

The troops set out on September 12, and the next day encamped within several miles of Fort Duquesne. Supremely confident, Grant directed Maj. Andrew Lewis to proceed to the fort about midnight with 400 men and "attack everything that was found about the fort." Lewis and his men returned about dawn. Having lost contact with one another in the night woods, they prudently decided to retire back to camp.

Grant then made another foolish move; he sent fifty of his Highlanders to attack an Indian camp near the fort. The soldiers did find the camp, but there were no Indians in it. They set fire to a storehouse and then withdrew.

After that, as related by historian Walter O'Meara, "Grant got the idea that the French were too weak to attempt a sally. Stationing himself on a rise of ground with 200 Highlanders, 100 Marylanders, and 100 Pennsylvanians, he sent 100 of the Highlanders with drums beating and pipes skirling, across the open ground—possibly to cut off a sortie from the garrison." It was now seven o'clock in the morning.

Warned in plenty of time, Capt. François-Marie de Ligneris, the commander at Fort Duquesne, opened the gates of the fort and sent out an attack force of French troops and Indians—perhaps as many as 800 men. They overwhelmed the Highlanders very quickly and drove back the Pennsylvanians and the remainder of Grant's troops. The only thing that prevented a wholesale massacre was the heroic action of the Virginian soldiers under Capt.

Thomas Bullit. The defeat was very costly—more than 300 men killed or captured. Major Grant himself was taken prisoner.

Several days after this resounding blow, Washington was summoned to Raystown to confer with General Forbes, who scolded him for his intemperate outbursts about the roads, and ordered him to bring the rest of his Virginia troops to Raystown immediately. Several weeks later they were ordered to proceed immediately to Loyal Hannon. Slogging their way through torrential rains for ten dreary days, the Virginians finally arrived at Loyal Hannon on October 23. Weak and suffering great pain from dysentery, General Forbes arrived a few days later, carried in a litter swung between two horses.

Writing to Francis Fauquier, Governor Dinwiddie's successor, Washington noted that "My march to this post gave me an opportunity of forming a judgement of the road, and I can truly say, that it is indiscribably bad. . . . The general and a great part of the troops, &c, being yet behind, and the weather growing very inclement, must I apprehend terminate our expedition for this year, at this place."

Washington's gloomy prediction—his whole military outlook in fact—was almost obsessively centered on Fort Duquesne only. To his mind, the war was going very badly, but unknown to him, several important developments were taking place in other areas that would prove very favorable to the British.

In August, British forces had attacked and destroyed the French Fort Frontenac on Lake Ontario, thus cutting Fort Duquesne's vital supply line from Montreal and Niagara. Immense quantities of ammunition and other supplies destined for the Forks were captured, as well as the French fleet which had defended the supply lines on the lake.

To add to French woes, many of their Indian allies were beginning to abandon them. For some months General Forbes and

Pennsylvania officials had been negotiating with the Indians, and in October a great council with the Delaware and other Eastern tribes was held at Easton, Pennsylvania—a council that successfully weaned the eastern Delaware Indians to the British side. Then a brave Moravian missionary, Christian Frederic Post, carried messages of peace and friendship to the Ohio Indians, some of them practically within sight of Fort Duquesne. Due to Post's efforts, and the influence of the eastern Delaware chief, Teedyuscung, many of the Ohio tribes abandoned their French ties and made peace with the British. The switch had come at a crucial time.

The French at Fort Duquesne still had Indian allies, however, and Captain de Ligneris began sending out small parties to make surprise attacks on the men building the Forbes road. Several scalps were taken. On October 12, de Ligneris sent out a sizeable force—440 Frenchmen and 150 Indians—to attack Fort Ligonier. The British and colonials left the fort to fight in the open, but eventually both sides broke off the engagement. The British had twelve dead, eighteen wounded, and thirty-one missing. That night the attacking force returned and stole most of the horses and cattle. The British spoke of the affair as a "victory," but it was not one at all.

On November 11, General Forbes held a council with his officers to decide on their next step. After weighing all options, and the advantages and disadvantages of pressing on to take Fort Duquesne that fall, he decided to hunker down and wait until spring for the attack on the fort.

The next day, British scouts raced into Fort Ligonier to report a large enemy force just three miles distant. To counter them, General Forbes sent out 500 Virginians under Lt. Col. John Mercer.

Hearing the loud sounds of battle, Washington got the general's permission to lead out a group of volunteers to help rout the foe. It was dusk and getting darker, so he sent scouts ahead to tell Mercer they were coming.

Musket shots sounded in front of them, and his men returned the fire. It was only when Washington heard familiar shouts in English ahead that he realized that it was Mercer and his Virginians. The two provincial parties were shooting at each other. Shouting for a cease fire, Washington then ran "between the two fires, knocking up with his sword the presented pieces."

Bullets whistled by on either side, and before the two groups could be made to understand, fourteen men were killed and twenty-six wounded. It had been a very costly mistake. Many years later, Washington wrote that his life that day had been "in as much jeopardy as it had ever been before or since."

Mercer had captured three prisoners during the action, and under sharp questioning they revealed that Fort Duquesne was in a weakened state, with few soldiers or Indian allies, and little food. This report, General Forbes wrote, "gives me great hope." Changing his mind, he decided that his army would forge ahead as speedily as possible. They would make Fort Duquesne theirs before the onset of winter.

18.

The Fall of Fort Duquesne

I have the pleasure to inform you that
Fort Duquesne . . . was possessed by his Majesty's
troops on the 25th instant.

— GEORGE WASHINGTON
Letter to Governor Fauquier

Putting his decision into action, General Forbes ordered a quick advance with 2,500 troops, each man carrying only a knapsack and a blanket, along with his musket and ammunition. Heavy artillery and nonessential supplies were left behind. A speedy advance was more important.

Engineers and ax men went ahead to chart and clear the road. George Washington, temporarily commissioned a brigadier general for this action, led the advance division, and Bouquet followed with the rearguard troops and light artillery.

When the attack force set out on November 15, Washington sent the Pennsylvanians in his brigade far ahead. They would build a temporary defensive position, a redoubt, at some suitable spot, while he and the main body of troops climbed Chestnut Ridge, following the crude path cleared by the road-builders.

After an advance of six miles, the so-called road came to an end. The route ahead was supposed to have been blazed, but the marks on the trees were few and far between. Under Washington's direction the next day, his troops cut trees and began to extend the road themselves. After two days of back-breaking toil they arrived at Bushy Run and finally reached the advance camp made by the Pennsylvanians.

Marching ahead with 1,000 men, Washington established another redoubt beyond Turtle Creek. He then cut back toward Bouquet's division behind him.

When they met, the army marched forward as a single force, with scouts on either side to warn of any French or Indians venturing forth to challenge them. By November 23 they were within twelve or fifteen miles of Fort Duquesne, and General Forbes ordered a halt. He wanted his scouts to check on conditions around the fort and report back to him before the final assault.

The army remained in camp the next day while the scouts were out spying on the enemy. Washington was anxious at the delay. The enlistment of his Virginians ended on December 1— just six more days. Could they take the fort before that date?

The next day one of the Indian scouts came into camp to say that he had seen "a very thick smoke . . . extending in the bottom along the Ohio." Soon there was more definite news, as Washington reported in a letter to Governor Fauquier on November 28. "Honble Sir: I have the pleasure to inform you, that Fort Duquesne, or the ground rather on which it stood, was possessed by his Majesty's troops on the 25th instant. The enemy, after letting us get within a day's march of the place, burned the fort and ran (by the light of it) at night, going down the Ohio by water, to the number of about five hundred men. . . . The possession of this fort has been a matter of surprise to the whole army. . . ."

When the British and colonial forces reached the Forks of the Ohio, they were confronted only by smoking ruins—the remains of Fort Duquesne and the burnt-out shells of thirty nearby cabins, with just their chimneys still standing. One of the powder magazines had not exploded, and it contained countless scalping knives. Many human bones lay scattered through the surrounding forest. The few Indians that remained nearby were eager to make peace. Colonel Bouquet counciled with them and gave them gifts.

Carried to the site on his litter, General Forbes ordered that a small stockaded fort be built at the Forks, to be manned during the winter by Lieutenant Colonel Mercer and 200 men. In the spring another, stronger fort would be built. It would be called Fort Pitt, after the great English statesman, and would be the biggest and most strongly defended fort in America.

The fall of Fort Duquesne—accomplished without a battle— was a notable victory for the British, for it severed French lines of communication on the Ohio, and isolated New Orleans. Even so, the French and Indian War was far from finished. There would be several more years of bloody conflict before the British and colonials celebrated final victory over the French. But as far as George Washington was concerned, the war was over. With the taking of Fort Duquesne and the neutralizing of the Indians, the frontiers of his beloved Virginia were at last secure. He let it be known that he would resign from the military.

The officers of the Virginia Regiment signed an address to Washington on December 31, 1758, imploring him to stay with them. "Your steady adherence to impartial Justice, your quick Discernment and invariable Regard to Merit . . . first heightened our natural Emulation, and our Desire to excel. . . . Judge then, how sensibly we must be Affected with the loss of such an excellent

Commander, such a sincere Friend, and so able a Companion. How rare it is to find those amiable Qualifications blended together in one Man? How great the loss of such a Man?"

Nonetheless, Washington bid farewell to his officers, replying, "It was really the greatest honor of my life to command gentlemen who made me happy in their company and easy in their conduct." He remained firm in his plan to leave.

On January 1, 1759, George Washington resigned his command. Five days later he married Martha Custis and returned with her to Mount Vernon to resume his life as a plantation owner. There he enjoyed many years of a peaceful gentleman's life before returning in 1776 to military duty as commander-in-chief of the Continental Army in the Revolutionary War against the British.

 *Epilogue*

As his [Washington's] ambition broadened,
it compassed four things—wealth, "honor,"
eminence, and military distinction.
— DOUGLAS SOUTHALL FREEMAN
George Washington: A Biography

When George Washington resigned his commission and returned to civilian life, he was still a young man—just twenty-six years old. In the summer of 1754, inexperienced and eager, he had heard bullets whistling around him and found "something charming in the sound." Not so five years later. His service in the French and Indian War had taught him a great deal about the trials, uncertainties, and limitations of command.

During those five years of military duty, he had experienced only several days of actual combat, and all of those combats had ended badly: the Jumonville affair in massacre; Fort Necessity in crushing defeat; Braddock's march in total disaster; and confused Virginians shooting at each other in the unfortunate skirmish at

Fort Ligonier. In all of these happenings, however, Washington had displayed a rare courage, and total disregard for personal safety, that few could match.

It was for these characteristics that he was a hero to his officers, and to Virginians of every class as well. After his resignation, the colony's General Assembly passed a resolution enthusiastically praising him. Yet he left the service with a fair amount of bitterness. He had never attained the status he had so devoutly wished— a commission as a regular British officer. He also considered that he had been treated unfairly by many of his superiors. He was not yet able to realize that many of the things he had done—or the *way* he had done them—were foolish or wrong-headed.

Whether he realized it or not, the day-to-day uncertainties and concerns of military life had taught Washington many things that would be invaluable to him in the future. Through the trials and tribulations of many frustrating months, he had learned a great deal about the inevitable difficulties of military administration. Vitally needed supplies of food, clothing, ammunition, transport, and medical help were almost always inadequate. By necessity he had learned how to save, how to do the best he could with what he had. He already had abundant self-confidence, and the ability to assume responsibility without question. As his biographer James Flexner noted, "He learned in the most difficult of all possible schools how to hold men by a combination of authority, violence, threats, persuasion, and inspiring leadership."

One of the hardest lessons he learned was the need to control his temper. Usually amiable and considerate, he earned the devotion of his officers, and always tried to deal with both the officers and common soldiers with absolute justice. He also learned the need for firm discipline in dealing with insolence, drunkenness, and desertion.

Washington had always had a strong sense of order, and put everything he had into every effort. He wanted to do his full duty.

Above all, his boundless effort to get ahead in life drove him to strive for perfection.

"His was the quenchless ambition of an ordered mind," observed biographer Douglas Southall Freeman. "Ambition was Washington through 1758; . . . As his ambition broadened, it compassed four things—wealth, 'honor,' eminence, and military distinction. All these might be stated in terms of the infinitive of ambition, which is to excel."

After retiring to Mount Vernon, Washington enjoyed sixteen peaceful years as owner and administrator of a large and prosperous plantation. He was happily married, an elected member of the Virginia Assembly, and enjoyed all the social pleasures and recreational pursuits of the prosperous Virginia gentry.

In his youth he had been an ardent Anglophile who thought of England as "home," with his beloved Virginia a proud offspring of the motherland. Yet during those peaceful years at Mount Vernon, his regard for England diminished in the wake of British laws and decrees which he considered unfair to the colonies. More and more, he thought of himself, first of all, as an American.

"Down the years Washington mulled over his experiences in the French and Indian War," Flexner observes. "As his character and world view expanded, new meanings became clear to him. He accurately defined his failures . . . and worked over the reasons why he had failed. The results of this protracted self-education were to prove of the greatest importance to the creation of the United States."

During those years, England continued to treat her American colonies as second-class children. Controlling and administering an empire that now covered much of North America was expensive, and the British parliament decreed that the colonies should pay part of the costs. Various products were taxed, eventually including tea, the favorite beverage of Englishmen and colonials.

The Americans deeply resented this "taxation without representa-
tion." Feelings went from bad to worse, culminating in the Boston
Tea Party of December 1773, when several hundred Massachusetts
patriots, disguised as Indians, boarded three British merchant ships
loaded with tea and dumped over 300 cases of it into the harbor.

In retaliation, Parliament passed the Intolerable Acts, closing
Boston to all shipping, with the British army present to enforce the
ruling. Inflamed, Virginia and the other colonies rallied to the
defense of the Bostonians. By now, George Washington was firm
in his opposition to the British position. "Shall we supinely sit and
see one province after another fall prey to despotism?" he wrote.

As a member of the Virginia Assembly, Washington voted for
a meeting of all the other colonies to consider what should be
done. He then went to Philadelphia as a delegate to the First
Continental Congress in 1774.

In April 1775 the British and colonials fought one another in
the battles of Concord and Lexington, firing "the shot heard
around the world." The die was cast, and full-scale warfare began.
In June Washington again traveled to Philadelphia as a delegate
to the Second Continental Congress. There he was unanimously
elected as commander-in-chief of the Continental Army that was
to combat the British for the next six years, until final victory was
theirs.

Everything Washington had experienced and learned during
the French and Indian War helped him in his maturity. When he
was called to lead the thirteen colonies in the War for Independence, he was ready.

Selected Bibliography

Unless otherwise noted in the text, all quotations in this book are taken from Washington's *Writings* and *Diaries* as edited by Fitzpatrick, or from Flexner and Freeman.

Alberts, Robert C. *A Charming Field for an Encounter. The Story of George Washington's Fort Necessity.* Washington, D.C.: Division of Publications, National Park Service, 1975

Anderson, Fred. *The Seven Year War and the Fate of Empire in British North America, 1754-1766.* New York: Alfred A. Knopf, 2000

Flexner, James Thomas. *George Washington: The Forge of Experience, 1732-1775.* Boston: Little Brown, 1965

———.*Washington, the Indispensible Man.* New York: New American Library, 1979

Freeman, Douglas Southall. *George Washington: A Biography.* Volumes 1 and 2. New York: Scribner's, 1948

Marrin, Albert. *George Washington & the Founding of a Nation.* New York: Dutton Children's Books, 2001

Morrison, Samuel Eliot. *The Young Man Washington.* Cambridge, Mass.: Harvard University Press, 1932

O'Meara, Walter. *Guns at the Forks.* Pittsburgh, Pa.: The University of Pittsburgh Press, 1979

Tebbel, John. *George Washington's America.* New York: E.P. Dutton, 1954

Washington, George. *The Diaries of George Washington.* Edited by John C. Fitzpatrick. Vol. 1, 1748-1770. Boston: Houghton Mifflin, 1925

———.*The Writings of George Washington from the Original Manuscript Sources.* Vol. 1, 1745-1756; Vol. 2, 1757-1769; Vol. 29, 1786-1788. Edited by John C. Fitzpatrick. Washington, D.C.: U.S. Government Printing Office, 1931 and 1939

Washington, George, and Christopher Gist. *A Reprint of the Journal of George Washington, and That of His Guide, Christopher Gist, Reciting Their Experiences on the Historic Mission from Governor Dinwiddie of Virginia, to the French Commandant at Fort Le Boeuf in November-December, 1753.* Edited and compiled by Don Marshall Larrabee. Williamsport, Pa.: Grit Publishing Co., 1924

Index

(Asterisks after page numbers indicate illustrations)

Alexandria (Va.), 9, 40
Algonquin Indians, 14
Aliquippa, Queen, 35, 53
Allegheny Mountains, 6, 9, 11, 102
Allegheny River, 6, 7, 12, 21, 34, 36
Amherst, Jeffery, 95
Anson, John (physician), 94

Barbados (West Indies), 5
Beaujeu, Daniel Liénard de, 71, 74
Bedford, Fort, 102
Blue Ridge Mountains, 5, 61, 82, 87
Boston (Mass.), 86, 114
Boston Tea Party, 114
Bouquet, Henry, 96-100, 102, 103, 107, 108, 109;
    quoted, 97-100
Braddock, Edward, 87, 90, 96;
    description of, 63-64, 79;
    makes Washington his aide, 61;
    his contempt for Indians, 56, 79;
    marches on Fort Duquesne, 66-71, 67*, 111;
    defeated by French and Indians, 71, 72-76, 72*-73*;
    wounded, 75-77, 77*;
    dies, 78;
    quoted, 78
Braddock Road, 95-100;
    map of, 98-99

Campbell, John. *See* Loudon, Fourth Earl of
Catawba Indians, 15, 85
Cayuga Indians, 13
Cherokee Indians, 85
Chestnut Ridge, 11, 108
Coldstream Guards, 63
Concord, Battle of, 114
Continental Army, 110, 114
Continental Congress, 95, 114
Contrecouer, Captain, 41, 48, 49, 71
Cresap, Thomas, 36
Croghan, George, 53, 56, 70, 71
Cumberland, Fort, 9, 66, 87, 90, 97, 102;
    defeated army at, 79, 80;
    conditions at, 83, 86, 88
Currin, Barnaby, 9, 12, 29
Custis, Martha, 94, 110

Dagworthy, John, 83, 86, 87, 88
Davison, John, 14, 23
Delaware Indians, 14, 23, 53, 56, 82, 105
Dinwiddie, Robert, 5, 6;
    sends Washington to warn the French, 7-8;
    text of his letter to the French, 27-28;

publishes Washington's journal, 37-38;
promotes Washington, 39, 83;
disagreements with Washington, 61, 62, 88, 91-92;
quoted 62, 81, 88, 91
Dumas, Jean-Daniel, 74
Dunbar, Thomas, 78, 79, 81
Duquesne, Fort, 42*, 52, 63, 81, 87, 90, 95, 96;
French build, 43;
Braddock marches on, 66-71, 67*;
Braddock's defeat before, 71-77;
Grant's raid on, 103-04;
Forbes marches on, 107-08;
burned by French, 108, 109
Duquesne, Marquis, 6, 29

Erie, Lake, 6, 11, 17, 22

Fairfax, Anne, 4
Fairfax, Thomas, 4, 5
Fairfax, William, 4
Fauquier, Francis, 104, 108
Ferry Farm, 4
Flexner, James Thomas, quoted, 1, 85, 112, 113
Forbes, John, 95-102, 104-09;
reprimands Washington, 100, 104;
quoted, 106
Forbes Road, 96-102, 104;
map of, 98-99
Forks of the Ohio: location of, 6, 12;
strategic importance of, 12;
Virginians build fort at, 39-41;
French build fort at, 43;
occupied by British, 108-09
Forts. *See* individual names

Franklin, Benjamin, 39;
cartoon by, 65*
Frazier, John, 11, 21, 35
Freeman, Douglas Southall, quoted, 3, 113
French Creek, 7, 18, 21, 22, 24, 25, 28
Frontenac, Fort, 104
Fry, Joshua, 39, 43, 54

Gage, Thomas, 70
George II (King of England), 5, 7, 63, 95; quoted, 7
George III (King of England), 40
George, Lake, 95
Gist, Christopher, 9, 10, 11, 21, 24, 35*, 36, 44, 53, 54;
accompanies Washington to the French, 9-35;
new settlement of 35, 56;
quoted, 32-34, 44
Gordon, Harry, 71
Grant, James, 102-04
Great Meadows, 11, 43, 48, 52-60, 89

Half-King (Tanacharisson), 14;
spokesman for the Iroquois, 12, 15;
tells of meeting with Marin, 16-18;
accompanies Washington to warn the French, 19-32;
joins Washington to attack the French, 44-45;
kills Jumonville, 47, 49-51;
at Fort Necessity, 53-57;
death of, 70;
quoted, 41, 54
Harris's Ferry, 97
Highlanders, 102-03

Hog, Peter, 40, 44, 47
House of Burgesses (Va.), 4, 101

Indians, 13-14, 17, 19, 104-05;
depredations of, 82, 83, 84*,
89. *See also* specific tribes
Innes, James, 54, 61
Intolerable Acts, 114
Iroquois Confederacy, 12, 13, 15
Iroquois Indians, 13, 21, 23, 70,
79

Jenkins, William, 9
Jeskakake, Chief, 19, 23
Joncaire, Philippe Thomas, 19, 21,
22, 23, 33
Jumonville Affair, 44-51, 52, 59,
60, 111
Jumonville, Joseph Coulon Sieur
de, 47, 48, 49-50, 58, 60

Kaninguen, Denis, 49
Kustaloga, Chief, 23

La Force, Monsieur, 23, 48
La Salle, Robert Cavalier, Sieur
de, 6, 22
Laurel Hill (Ridge), 11, 43, 101,
102
Le Boeuf, Fort, 7, 11, 16, 18, 22,
23, 24, 37, 49, 50;
Washington visits, 25-30;
description of, 28
Lexington, Battle of, 114
Ligneris, François-Marie de, 103,
105
Ligonier, Fort, 102, 105, 112
Logstown (Pa.), 9, 14, 21
Loudoun, Fort, 89
Loudoun, Fourth Earl of, 89, 90,
95
Louis XIV (King of France), 6

Louis XV (King of France), 28
Louisburg (Canada), 95
Louisiana, 6
Lowinolach, Chief, 14
Loyal Hannon, 101, 102, 103,
104

Machault, Fort, 7
Mackay, James, 55, 56, 59
MacQuire, John, 9
Marin, Pierre Paul, 11, 22, 24;
quoted, 16-17
Mercer, John, 105-06, 109
Miami Indians, 14
Militia, Virginia, 4, 5, 36, 39, 40;
poor performance of, 85, 87-
89
Mingo Indians, 56, 71
Mississippi River, 6
Mohawk Indians, 13, 79
Monakatoocha, Chief, 14, 18-19
Monongahela River, 7, 11, 12,
39, 41, 69, 81
Montcalm, General, 94
Montreal (Canada), 16, 22, 104
Morrison, Samuel Eliot, quoted,
2
Mount Vernon, 4, 63, 65, 94,
110, 113
Murthering Town (Pa.), 20, 33

Necessity, Fort, 56;
description of, 53-54*;
fall of, 57-60, 61, 64, 94, 111
New France, 6, 29, 43, 87
New Orleans (La.), 109
Niagara, Fort, 104

Ohio Company, 6, 36, 43 55, 96;
description of, 5;
strong house at Wills Creek,
9;

storehouse at Redstone Creek, 43, 60
Ohio, Forks of. *See* Forks of the Ohio
Ohio River, 5, 7, 9, 12, 14, 22
Ohio Valley, 6, 7, 18, 22, 29, 60
O'Meara, Walter, quoted, 82, 103
Oneida Indians, 13
Onondaga Indians, 13
Ontario, Lake, 6, 22, 95, 104
Oswego, Fort, 22, 95

Parliament, British, 95, 113, 114
Peale, Charles Willson, ii
Philadelphia (Pa.), 79, 81, 90, 95, 114
Pitt, Fort, 109
Pitt, William (Earl of Chatham), 95, 96
Post, Christian Frederic, 105
Potomac River, 4, 65
Presque Isle, Fort, 6, 7, 17, 27
Prince George, Fort, 40, 41

Quebec (Canada), 6, 29

Raystown (Pa.), 100, 102, 104
Redstone Creek, 41, 55, 60
Revolutionary War, American, 1, 85, 110

Scarroyady, Chief, 56, 70; quoted, 79
Seneca Indians, 12, 13, 14, 15, 21
Sharpe, Horatio, 62, 63, 87; quoted, 81
Shaw, Jim, quoted, 49-50
Shawnee Indians, 14, 56
Shenandoah Valley, 9, 82, 87
Shingiss, Chief, 14
Shirley, William, 86, 87, 88
Stephen, Adam, 59, 83; quoted, 58

Steward, Henry, 9, 12
St. Lawrence River, 95
St. Pierre, Legardeur de, 27, 28, 37
Stobo, Robert, 42, 59
Susquehanna River, 82

Tanacharisson, Chief. *See* Half-King
Teedyuscung, Chief, 105
Treaty belts, 17, 18, 19, 23, 29
Trent, William, 36, 39, 40, 41
Turtle Creek, 11, 108
Tuscarora Indians, 13

Van Braam, Jacob, 8, 21, 33, 40, 59
Venango (Pa.), 7, 11, 15, 19-24, 29, 30, 32, 33, 51
Villiers, Coulon de, 59; quoted, 57, 58
Virginia Assembly, 39, 86, 88, 95, 112, 113, 114
Virginia Regiment, 49, 55, 62, 83, 87, 90, 94, 95, 109

Walpole, Horace, quoted, 51
War for Independence, 114
Ward, Edward, 40, 41
Washington, Augustine (father), 3-4
Washington, Augustine Jr. (half-brother), 4
Washington, George, ii*;
    early years, 3-5;
    journey to the French, 7-36, 21*;
    map of journey, 26, 35*;
    and the Jumonville affair, 44-51;
    and the Fort Necessity campaign, 52-60;
    and the Braddock campaign, 65-80;

and the Forbes campaign, 93-109

Washington, Jack (brother), 48, 68, 75

Washington, Lawrence (half-brother), 3-5, 63

Weems, Mason, quoted, 2

White Thunder, Chief, 19, 23, 32

William Henry, Fort, 95

Williamsburg (Va.), 5, 29, 36, 60, 61, 63, 86, 87, 94

Wills Creek, 9, 10, 11, 40, 60

Winchester (Va.), 9, 53, 87, 93, 94;

Washington builds fort at, 88-89

Wyandot Indians, 14

Youghiogheny River, 11, 43, 68